I REMEMBER NOTHING MORE

I REMEMBER NOTHING MORE

*The Warsaw Children's Hospital
and the Jewish Resistance*

Adina Blady Szwajger

❖   ❖   ❖

TRANSLATED FROM THE POLISH BY
TASJA DAROWSKA AND DANUSIA STOK

Pantheon Books *New York*

Library of Congress Cataloging-in-Publication Data

Blady Szwajger, Adina, 1917–
I remember nothing more: the Warsaw Children's Hospital and
the Jewish resistance/Adina Blady Szwajger; translated from
the Polish by Tasja Darowska and Danusia Stok.   p.   cm.
1. Blady Szwajger, Adina, 1917–   . 2. Jews—Poland—Warsaw—
Biography. 3. Physicians, Jewish—Poland—Warsaw—Biography.
4. Holocaust, Jewish (1939–1945)—Poland—Warsaw—Personal
narratives. 5. Warsaw Children's Hospital. 6. World War,
1939–1945—Underground movements, Jewish—Poland—
Warsaw. 7. Zydowska Organizacja Bojowa (Poland) 8. Warsaw
(Poland)—Biography. I. Title.
DS135.P63B543   1991   940.53'18'094384—dc20
ISBN 0-679-40034-6   90-53402

❖ ❖ ❖ ❖ ❖

CONTENTS

v

CONTENTS

✧ ✧ ✧ ✧ ✧

ILLUSTRATIONS

documents she lost in the Gestapo raid on the café in Miodowa street.

The author's *Kennkarte* (identity card) in the name of Irena Mereminska issued by the General Government of Poland under German occupation on 27 July 1943 and due for renewal on 27 July 1948.

Membership card of the Warsaw–Bialystock Medical Association, accrediting the author as a qualified doctor.

Home Army identity card.

The monument to the Heroes of the Warsaw Ghetto.

ILLUSTRATIONS IN TEXT

Page 173

The temporary pass issued by Dr W. Skonieczny in his capacity as Regional Medical Officer of North Warsaw, which allowed the author and thirteen companions to escape from the city after the collapse of the Warsaw Uprising.

Page 173

Certificate issued by the Home Army on 3 October 1944.

Page 176

A record of Jewish children placed with Aryan families recovered from the rubble in the basement of a destroyed house.

❖ ❖ ❖ ❖ ❖

CHRONOLOGY

1917	Adina Blady Szwajger born to Icchak Blady Szwajger and Stefania Szwajger (née Hertzberg).
1933	Begins degree course at the Faculty of Medicine of the University of Warsaw.
27 July 1939	Marries Stefan Szpigielman. Ten-day honeymoon in Ustronie
8–29 August	Spends three weeks as instructor at a school summer camp in Kazimierz on the Vistula.
	Nazi Soviet Non-Aggression Treaty signed by Ribbentrop and Molotov.
30 August	Adina returns to Warsaw.
1 September 1939	German invasion of Poland. At that time 3.5 million Jews are living in Poland, of whom 393,950 live in Warsaw, constituting one third of its population.
4 September	Adina's classes at the university terminated as credited.
6 September	Colonel Umiastowski announces on the radio that Warsaw will be an open city; all men able to carry arms are ordered to leave. Later it is decided to defend the city.

During the Siege of Warsaw Adina works in a dressing station in Swietojerska street.

17 September   Soviet invasion of Poland.

21 September   Conference in Berlin, chaired by Reinhard Heydrich, Chief of the Reich Central Security Office, decides the fate of Polish Jewry.

28 September   Capitulation of Warsaw. German occupation begins.

11 October   Adina goes to Lvov in the Soviet zone via Bialystok, where she meets up with Stefan, hoping to complete her studies at Jan Kazimierz University. Stays in Lvov until December.

1939–40   Resettlement and ejection of Jews. Beginning of the ejection of Jews from the so-called Warthegau (the territories of western Poland annexed to the Reich) with the exception of Lodz. The first ghetto is established in Piotrkow in October 1939. In February 1940 the Jews from Lodz, the second-largest Jewish community, are enclosed in a ghetto.

October 1939   Enclosure of the main Jewish areas in Warsaw with barbed wire.

November   Decree ordering the formation of a *Judenrat*, a Council of Jewish Elders, to administer the ghetto. Its members have to be approved by German authorities. Jews are ordered to wear Star of David armbands outside the ghetto.

December   Large signs declaring "Danger: Epidemic Zone" are put up by the Germans at entrance to the Jewish area.

End December Adina is warned that she is on a list for deportation to the Gulag and immediately decides to return to Warsaw. She is caught by a Soviet army patrol "smuggling" herself across the Nazi–Soviet border near Malkinia station, but escapes and reaches Warsaw after five days.

Spring 1940 Orders restricting movements between the Jewish area and the rest of Warsaw. Imposition of forced labour.

11 March Adina starts work in the Bersohn and Bauman Children's Hospital in Sienna street; appointed to the TB Ward on Sliska street, now in the "little ghetto".

November The ghetto is closed, with nearly half a million Jews living behind its walls.

26 June 1941 Adina contracts typhus while visiting a displaced persons' camp, and is seriously ill until early August.

September–October Adina works in the newly opened branch of the Children's Hospital on Leszno street.

November Introduction of death penalty for Jews caught leaving the ghetto illegally and for Poles caught helping them. Conditions of life in the ghetto are extremely hard. The daily food ration is 184 calories. Eleven thousand Jews die of hunger in 1941 (typhus causing 15 per cent of deaths).

22 July 1942 First mass deportations from the ghetto ordered. Germans claim that all Jews are to be resettled in the east, except for those employed by the *Judenrat*, German workshops, Jewish police, Jewish hospital staff and their immediate families.

23 July	Adam Czerniakow, head of the *Judenrat*, commits suicide.
30 July	Adina's mother, Stefania (Bat-Sheva) Hertzberg-Szwajger, and other Yehudia teachers deported to the death camp at Treblinka.
July–September	Main wave of deportations to the death camp at Treblinka. The *Judenrat* has to deliver at first 6,000, then 10,000 Jews daily to the *Umschlagplatz*, from where allegedly they are to be resettled in work camps, but in reality they are taken to Treblinka.
	Adina attempts to commit suicide, but is saved by Dr Hela Keilson.
	The Children's Hospital is closed and relocated on Stawki street on the *Umschlagplatz*.
	Adina mercifully gives morphine to the last surviving children in the hospital as the Germans and Szaulis begin taking the sick from the other wards to the cattle trucks.
September 1942	The ghetto given the status of a work camp. Only 60,000 Jews are left in the ghetto.
	Formation of ZOB (Jewish Fighting Organization).
October 1942–January 1943	Adina is given a "life ticket" and, with other colleagues from the Hospital, begins work in a makeshift hospital in Gesia street.
December 1942	Foundation of Zegota (Council for Aid to Jews) by the Polish government in exile to help Jews to escape from the ghetto.

January 1943	The first armed Jewish resistance initiated by ZOB. Szlengel writes the poem "Counterattack" to commemorate it.
	Hospital on Gesia street closed by the Gestapo. Adina and thirty others successfully conceal themselves in a hiding place on the second floor of the building and survive.
25 January	Adina leaves the ghetto with false papers, and lives in room on Dzielna street until it is "burned" following a raid on the ZOB café in Miodowa street during the Ghetto Uprising. Right up until the Warsaw Uprising in August 1944 she works as a courier for ZOB, distributing large sums of money to those in hiding, finding safe houses, arranging false documents, providing medical care, etc.
19 April 1943	The Ghetto Uprising. The final attempt to liquidate the remaining inhabitants of the ghetto is met by force. The uneven battle lasts three weeks. Seven thousand Jews are killed in the fighting, 6,000 burn to death in their hideouts and 56,000 are transported to Treblinka. Some of the surviving fighters escape through the sewers and are taken by lorry into hiding in the forest.
11 July 1943	Stefan, worn down by months of living in hiding, believing he is buying his way out to Switzerland, falls into the "Hotel Poland" trap – the lorries go straight to Auschwitz – Adina narrowly escapes.
Summer 1943	Adina lives in Miedzylesie during the summer, and in the room at 24 Miodowa street during the winter.

Winter 1943–44	Works as a childminder in the RGO Hall, while continuing her resistance work.
29 July 1944	Adina and Marysia (Bronka Feinmesser) leave the Miedzylesie flat to be in Warsaw for the Uprising.
1 August 1944 *2 October*	The Warsaw Uprising: an attempt to liberate Warsaw, prior to the arrival of the Soviet Army. In the fighting 150,000–200,000 civilians and 10,000 Home Army and other soldiers lose their lives; Warsaw is razed to the ground.
29 September	Wik Slawski (Wladyslaw Swidowski, later Adina's second husband) helps the survivors of the Hospital set up during the Uprising to escape through the sewers from the Old Town to the centre of Warsaw.
2 October 1944	Collapse of the Warsaw Uprising.
11 October	Adina obtains a doctor's pass, a nurse's pass, and twelve passes for the wounded from the Red Cross hospital. In this way some of the survivors of the hospital escape from Warsaw. Adina and Wladek take a flat in Grodzisko above a unit of German gendarmes who are looking for resistance fighters, and set out to find the rest of their ZOB friends. In November they are successful.
17 January 1945	Liberation of Warsaw by the Soviet Army.
18 January 1945	Soviet and Polish troops liberate Grodzisko; Adina and friends return to Warsaw.
25 January	Adina begins work with the Main Committee of Polish Jews, finding Jewish children placed with Aryan families during the war.

15 May 1945 Adina moves to Lagiewniki, near Lodz, to take up a post in a sanatorium under the supervision of Dr Anna Margolis (formerly Head of the TB Ward in the Bersohn and Bauman Hospital in the ghetto), and there begins her postwar work as a paediatrician specializing in chest diseases.

MAP 1 Administrative divisions in occupied Poland, 6 November 1940

MAP 2   Administrative divisions in occupied Poland, 1 September 1942

% of Jewish population in 1939

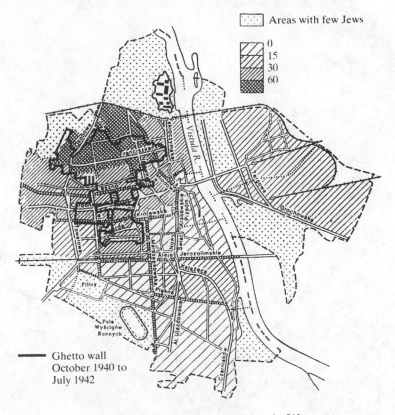

MAP 3 The location of the ghetto in Warsaw

MAP 4 The Warsaw ghetto

Boundary of the ghetto as set in
October 1940

Area from which Jews were
removed in 1942 and which
was left empty

Footbridge connecting 'large'
and 'small' ghettos

Gates (Wache)

Judenrat buildings

Tłomacka synagogue and library

Vistula River

I REMEMBER NOTHING MORE

❖ ❖ ❖ ❖ ❖

INTRODUCTION

I have myself to blame that only now am I writing when so many years have passed and so many things have faded from my memory. But immediately after the war I decided not to write any more. Never. What had happened wasn't something to be written about, or read; at least, that's what I thought. And to write about other, everyday, prewar matters didn't make sense. So – better nothing. And maybe I thought – had a faint hope – that if I remained silent, I'd manage to forget at least some of it and be able to live like everybody else. I don't know. Years were passing. I didn't manage to forget but I still believed that I had the right to remain silent. Yet I read everything written about the age of the gas chambers and realized more and more clearly that something wasn't quite right.

Many of those who had managed to survive the holocaust wrote about their experiences. In shattering words, they described the ghetto, that hell on earth, that most vile of the vilest concentration camps in which people weren't even necessarily killed – they simply died.

And there was no need for selection – everyone was condemned. Others wrote about how they managed to save lives, their own lives. And then, in the warmest words, they wrote about those who had helped them, saving not only human life but also their own human dignity.

Did I really have nothing to add?

I knew increasingly well that I did have something else to say, that it was necessary, that I ought to put across at least a fragment of the truth about all those in the ghetto who had never doubted as to how Man should live and die, or those who had never been tempted to escape; about those who will never say another word about themselves because their ashes have been scattered by the wind, who died at their posts trying to help others who were dying; not least about the "people in white", about the hospital.

And there's something else I ought to relate because that's what I know most about. Despite some accounts from the Aryan side,* nothing, or nearly nothing, is known about how those few fighters who had survived the horrors continued to live on the other side of the wall.

Yes, something is even known about the fact that the ghetto fighters who didn't die in the Ghetto Uprising continued to fight in the forests and in the Warsaw Uprising. But nowhere has it been told that when the struggle for the honour of dying came to an end, the struggle for survival began – not one's own survival, but the survival of those few (dozens? thousands?) hidden in Warsaw and other towns.

It was a difficult struggle.

Marek Edelman and Icchak Cukierman (the only two of the ZOB† Command who survived), as well as individual fighters who were more or less effectively hidden away, with a handful of couriers grouped around them, took upon them-

* Aryan side: here the author is referring to the non-Jewish Polish resistance. Elsewhere in the text the phrase "Aryan side" refers to the world outside the ghetto walls.

† Zydowska Organizacja Bojowa (Jewish Fighting Organization): set up in the autumn of 1942 in an attempt to organize an armed defence, ZOB's main aim was to train fighters and to obtain weapons and ammunition. The organization was led by Mordechaj Anielewicz (1920–43). The first armed conflict occurred in January 1943 (see Wladyslaw Szlengel's poem "Counterattack" on p. 69). Those who survived the Ghetto Uprising continued fighting in the Polish resistance.

selves the huge task of saving people. Just like Zegota,* of which everybody has heard.

Yes, it was a difficult struggle for ZOB. Their task was more difficult than that of any other underground organization. Endangered twice over (because of their stand against their oppressors and because of their racial descent), slipping through the streets where their own faces were their enemy and could sentence them to death, they bore on their shoulders responsibility for all those helpless and terrified "ordinary people" locked away and unable to move, waiting for help. And not just financial help. There were breakdowns, messy entanglements of different and frequently tragic incidents, diseases which had to be treated and deaths which had to be concealed. There was despair and hope. And anguish. Informers and people of good will. You had to be there at all times. It was hard. And then there was your own fear which could never be revealed. But it was there, coiled up tight, like a spring in your stomach. It would sometimes awake and send a piercing, icy shiver through your whole body.

It was there. You couldn't hide the fact.

Yet you had to – despite the fear.

And so I began to understand that although I didn't remember everything or know of everything, I had to speak out. But still I hung back. Still I resisted. Until another fear came over me. That I wouldn't make it in time. That I wouldn't repay the debt I owed to those times.

I had grown old. Sick. I lay in hospital. In a ward where, through the medium of the doctor in charge, I was constantly in the presence of the past.

And I started to hurry. There, on a hospital bed, I started to write. Quickly. To win the race against time. To make it

* Zegota: a cryptonym for the Council for Aid to Jews, an organization created by the Polish government in exile's plenipotentiary in Warsaw (Delegatura Rzadu) in December 1942 to help Jews to escape from the ghetto, to organize papers and money, and to find them shelter.

in time. Even if incompletely, fragmentarily, through the prism of my own incomplete memories. So, even though I know there are many things I can't remember and many I never knew, in this incomplete but truthful way I will try to recount something.

But first a few words about how things stood at the beginning, at the beginning of the war.

*   *   *

On 1 September 1939, the day war broke out, I was twenty-two, a student in her sixteenth term at the Faculty of Medicine at Warsaw University, and for exactly six weeks – since 27 July 1939 – I had been a married woman. Stefan and I were married but not living together. His parents were against the union of two students – Stefan was a third-year Law student – who had no money, nowhere of their own to live, and whose future held nothing but the tedious prospect of struggling to make ends meet. But we were in a hurry. We didn't want to wait for "stabilization". Besides, that academic year, 1939–40, I was to get my degree and doctor's licence. I wanted to have my husband's name on the diploma so as to avoid the formalities of changing my name, especially on my doctor's licence.

The fact that to get your doctor's licence you had to present a document stating your citizenship was also important. I could have had problems since my father, who had been living in Palestine for many years, was stateless – a refugee from Russia, with a Nansen passport.* Being married to a Polish citizen enabled me to avoid these complications. That's why we decided to have a quiet wedding, without informing either his parents or my mother, who suspected this would

---

* Nansen passport: a passport issued to stateless persons by the League of Nations after World War I. Named after Fridtjof Nansen (1861–1930), a Norwegian Arctic explorer, statesman and scientist, who was the League of Nation's high commissioner for refugees (1920–22) and who won the Nobel Peace Prize in 1922.

happen anyway. After the ceremony, which was performed by a "civilian rabbi" – the army chaplain – we went to my place and it turned out that my mother was waiting for us with a cake and bottle of wine. My aunt came with her son, whom I'd told over the telephone: "Jurek," I'd said, "come for a glass of wine, if you like – I've just got married." Such was the wedding. That same evening, we went off for a ten-day "holiday" in Ustronie. We had just enough money to spend those ten days "pretending (as we'd decided) to be rich". We were seen off to the station by Stefan's older brother, Mietek, himself a doctor who had already got his degree a year earlier.

We got back from Ustronie at the beginning of August. Stefan went back to his parents and prepared for his autumn exams. I went off for three weeks as an instructor at a school summer camp in Kazimierz on the Vistula.

I got back by boat on 29 August with anxious and frightened children, and that same day I went back to Kazimierz to fetch some of the children's luggage which there hadn't been room for on the boat.

I finally found myself in Warsaw on the evening of 30 August. Mamma wasn't back from her holidays yet. Trains were already being delayed. Conscription notices were posted in the streets of Warsaw. Windows were taped with strips of paper. Terrified people ran through the streets, buying whatever they could, hoarding up stocks of food. I, of course, didn't have any money. I had yet to be paid for the summer camp. Mamma came back on 31 August, also without money. She was due to get her wages – she was headmistress at the "Yehudia"* – the next day. Between us, we had just enough to buy a half-pound bar of Plutos chocolate.

---

* Yehudia: a private Jewish secondary school for girls, founded shortly before World War I, whose educational policy aimed to combine Zionist principles with a more general curriculum. The author's mother, Stefania (Bat-Sheva) Hertzberg-Szwajger, was Headmistress. After the destruction of the school during the battle for Warsaw in 1939, she and her colleagues continued to teach clandestinely until they were deported to Treblinka on 30 July 1942.

On 1 September, I was woken at dawn by a "rumbling". A storm? I tried to turn over. But already I heard the wail of a siren and, after a while, the speaker's voice over the radio – "Today at five o'clock in the morning" – Mamma came into my room – she was pale – crying – war . . .

That same 1 September, at eight in the morning, I joined my colleagues at the Hospital of the Bonifrater Fathers* to begin our psychiatric training. Professor Mazurkiewicz was there. Half of the boys were missing from our group of twenty-five. They had been called up. The professor calmly took the classes, several times interrupted by air raid warnings. Yes, those were the words – "Attention! Attention! Here it comes. Comma. Three . . .† I announce an air raid warning for the city of Warsaw . . ."

Despite danger, which was growing all around, despite shattered glass on the streets, despite the first ruins and the first wounded, the classes continued until 4 September.

At the end of that day, the professor said: "As from tomorrow the hospital is under military control. I dismiss you and consider the classes as credited. Leave your registration books to be signed, and see you after the war."

So we left the clinic and started our wild goose chase around the hospitals and temporary first-aid stations. But they didn't need us anywhere. I don't know whether this was the case only with us Jewish students – we moved around in a threesome – or whether in that terrible chaos of the *Blitzkrieg* everybody everywhere had lost their heads. At any rate, they didn't want us.

I went home. In the yard I met a neighbour, a nurse. She, too, hadn't been "assigned" anywhere. We quickly came to an understanding. In a corner of the temporary shelter which had been set up in the basement of our block at 30 Swietojerska street, we organized a "dressing station". I must admit that there were no problems when we "registered" at the

* A psychiatric clinic.
† Comma. Three: code words for the anti-aircraft defence.

6

nearest centre – on Freta street – and we received some dressings, a sterilizer and a set of basic instruments such as scalpel, forceps, even needles, thread and "nippers" for extracting stitches. I spent practically the whole three weeks of the Warsaw siege at that station. Popping upstairs to the apartment from time to time so as to get changed or eat something. During the first week, Mamma went to the school on Dluga street. Then classes were stopped so that the girls wouldn't have to walk through the streets, and she came with me to help in the shelter.

Stefan left Warsaw with all the men on the orders of Umiastowski.* He went east. In that shelter, I had my "baptism" of wartime working conditions. There, in a corner by the door, I delivered a baby – luckily it delivered itself. There, too, a fifteen-year-old boy died in my arms – a neighbour's son, hit by shrapnel during the terrible bombing of the Jewish district on Yom Kippur – 13 September 1939. From there we'd run to dig out the wounded from under rubble and sometimes we'd drag out only remains, sometimes shocked and wounded people. Our house survived. A shell tore out a window and a section of the wall of our apartment but nobody was there at the time. We could cope with life under siege. We were prepared to live through three times as much provided there was no surrender. That's what everybody felt that terrible day when we listened to Mayor Starzynski's last speech.† But Warsaw couldn't defend itself any longer. I stood amongst the crowds on Krakowskie Przedmiescie and watched the Germans march in. The crowds were so quiet you could hear the buzzing of a fly. Pale, drawn faces. And silent tears. The night of occupation had begun.

* On 6 September 1939, Colonel Umiastowski, a spokesman for the Warsaw military command, announced over the radio that Warsaw was to be an open city and that all men able to carry arms were to leave. Only later was it decided to defend the city.

† Stefan Starzynski (1893–1943): the heroic Mayor of Warsaw who organized the defence of the city; presumed to have died in a Nazi death camp.

At the beginning of October, a couple of colleagues and I went to the faculty offices. There, we found out two things. On the one hand, the Dean's secretary, jumping from a first-floor window of the burning university building, had saved the list of sixth-year students – we received certificates confirming that we had completed our studies and we were credited one month's classes which we hadn't finished. On the other hand, the Dean appointed by the Germans, "our" Professor Lauber, informed us: "What for you is the invader is for me the fatherland. And don't even think about passing exams. We won't be needing Polish, let alone Jewish doctors." With that, the three of us left.

We had to think what to do next.

Quite a large group of Polish and Jewish colleagues gathered at the faculty offices. We arranged to meet in two days time. At that meeting, we decided that the only way out was to go to Lvov, where "apparently" the Jan Kazimierz University was still open, and where we would be able to finish our studies. We didn't know much about what had happened on 17 September 1939.* And we certainly didn't understand much of it. At the time, we knew that Soviet troops had entered our country; there were even rumours that they were coming with help. Later, we heard about some sporadic defensive fighting, and about the fact that an order had been given not to resist. We didn't know anything about the Ribbentrop–Molotov Pact. Nor about the internment of our officers.† There were rumours that "there" (i.e. in Bialystok, Vilno and Lvov), life was practically normal and

---

* 17 September 1939: the Nazi–Soviet Non-Aggression treaty, signed in August 1939 and known as the Ribbentrop–Molotov Pact, contained a secret clause concerning the division of spheres of interest, which resulted in the Soviet attack on eastern Poland on 17 September 1939.

† Fifteen thousand Polish officers captured by the Red Army were sent to camps in the Smolensk area. About 4,500 officers from the Kozielsk camp were found by the Germans in a mass grave in the Katyn forest in 1943. The other graves remain undiscovered.

that the border was open, so we would be able to go there
and back. I didn't take long to think it over. Mamma also
thought I ought to go. Besides, I hoped I'd find Stefan, who
hadn't come back and so, I thought, must still be on the
other side. The decision was made. On 11 October, with my
friend Ewa Pat, her mother and my cousin Boris Szwajger,
I left Warsaw in a cart. There were a few others with us on
that cart who also wanted to cross the border.

On 13 October, I was in Bialystok. I met Stefan almost
immediately. It wasn't difficult. There were so many people
we knew. Almost all from Warsaw. On 15 October, we
filled in a questionnaire. One of the questions was: "Do
you intend to go back to Poland after the war or to stay
in the Soviet Union?" Obviously, the majority answered
that they were going back to Poland. In that way they
sealed their fate.

The fate of deportees. All those who answered like that
were sent, several months later, to the Gulag. My answer
was the same. But I didn't go to the depths of Russia. I
managed to escape even though I didn't quite realize the
danger of deportation.

*　　　*　　　*

Though I remember little of interest about the next few
months in Lvov, I do remember swarms of "fugitives",
meagre provisions, chaotic attempts at studying, exams taken
really only as a matter of form and constantly listening out
for news from "that side" and, finally, escape. The fact that
I managed to leave in time I owe – something never explained
– to a colleague, a Ukrainian from Lvov. I don't know
why but that day he approached me at the university and
whispered: "Go – I've seen your name on the list of deportees." I didn't go back to where I was staying with my
cousin and her son and, just as I stood, without anything
and in my worst clothes, I went to the station and left for
Bialystok. I urged my cousin to go with me. She didn't want

to. She didn't believe it. I went alone. The next day, they took her and her one-and-a-half-year-old child. Miraculously, they survived the far north.

The border was closed. You had to "smuggle" yourself out of the country. No, I didn't realize the danger I was in. I remember only a feeling of boundless horror at not returning to Poland, at staying in Russia away from Mamma and my country. I was – we were – even so naïve as to think that, after waiting out the period of "deportations", we'd be able to go back and finish our studies. That's why Stefan stayed on in Bialystok for a while. He was to get the feel of the situation and follow me or wait for my return. We thought that the journey would be safer for a woman. Of course, returning to Lvov proved to be impossible. Stefan came back to Warsaw a few days after me. We were happy to be together again.

My colleagues were deported. Many never returned.

But what was in store for us was no better.

All this took place at the end of December 1939. My journey back took five days. Apparently they were shooting at fugitives on the river Bug where the border ran between lands occupied by the Russians and those annexed by Germany. It was better to go through the fields, by Malkinia station. So that's how I went and was immediately caught by a Russian patrol. I explained that I was going to Warsaw to get my mother. Nobody cared, of course, and I was locked up in a pigsty. I can't remember how I escaped from that place stinking of dung but I do know that the following day I was free again, wandering somewhere near the station at Czeremcha – still on the other side of the border. I was hungry, dirty, short of sleep and frozen. I never discovered the identity of the man who helped me. I don't even know his name. He told me to pretend I was his wife and not to talk in Polish because Byelorussians – the inhabitants of Czeremcha were Byelorussians – didn't exactly love Poles and lost no time in turning them over to the police.

We went into a house. My companion spoke Byelorussian

fluently. I don't know what he told them but the fact is that we were given some scrambled eggs, a basin of water to wash our hands and faces in, and a bed covered with a red check eiderdown. That night we both slept in that bed under the same eiderdown and it didn't even occur to me that I was in bed (albeit almost fully dressed – bedbugs) with a strange man, or any man for that matter. In the morning, we had some tea and a slice of bread and my companion saw me off to the forest where fugitives were waiting for nightfall. There we said goodbye and I arranged to go on with a group of smugglers.* It was the only way to get across the illegal border because the smugglers, constantly going over and back, knew the way and the habits of the guards. I spent that day at the edge of the forest. I was hungry. At one point I noticed a group of people gathering around a woman wrapped in sheepskins – she was selling soup in dirty mugs which were being passed around. It tasted wonderful. The worst thing was trying to find the so-called privy, the little house with the heart.† Finally, my nose led me to the right place. My illegal crossing very nearly came to an end with my drowning in sh. . . But I got out in one piece, except for losing a glove – it was hard to reach down for it. Well, I still had my muff.

Finally, night fell and we started to make our way forward. Of course, my "travelling companions" forged ahead without looking back at me. I lost them quite quickly and found myself alone in a field at night. I heard shooting somewhere to the side. I was extremely frightened but stubbornly went on. At one point I fell into a stream? A huge puddle? I don't know. Thin ice cracked underfoot and I sank almost to my knees. I waded out but immediately a second pair of shoes formed on my feet – shoes made of ice. Somehow I managed

* As soon as the border was closed, smuggling began: food, moonshine, tobacco.

† In Poland, at that time, outside lavatories were common. The door had a little heart-shaped, glassless window let into it, hence the nickname.

not to get frostbite – probably thanks to that stubborn, incessant race forward.

When the sun rose, I discovered I was on the "right" side of the border. German signs – posters, some kind of *Bekanntmachungen** – and finally uniforms, German soldiers. I was in "Poland" . . .

I took a train to Warsaw and the first thing I actually remember was the walk home across Castle square. Castle square, from where my journey had begun two months earlier, stuck in my mind because I saw a shop on the corner of Miodowa street – a baker's shop – with rolls in the window. Of course I didn't have any money but I saw rolls . . . Real rolls . . . On the streets, people wrapped up in all kinds of shawls, walking quickly, and soldiers. I don't know any more, I didn't see.

I don't remember how I managed to drag myself to Swietojerska street. But from the yard I looked up at the windows of our apartment and saw the terrified face of my mother who, at the sight of me, clasped her head in her hands.

"Why did you come back?" was my welcome.

But later there was water to wash in, food, lots of food, and a bed – my own.

There really was a lot of food at home. A striking change in the habits of Warsaw residents since September – stocking up? Running away from a currency which now had practically no value? – and, above all, the memory of hunger which seemed to increase the need for food and for stocking up. And there was still milk, cheese and meat coming in from the country.

That's how my wartime stay in Warsaw began.

Stefan returned a few days after me, having taken the same route somewhat more smoothly. It was senseless to keep our marriage secret from his parents any longer. The war had changed their attitude to the premature union of two students.

---

* *Bekanntmachungen*: proclamations concerning public regulations put up by the German Army.

So we settled down together in our apartment and before we could make any further decisions, I fell ill. It began with an "innocent" toothache which turned out to be an abscess. Several months of going hungry had lowered my resistance and I collapsed with a serious infection – two incisions of the abscess and so on. This lasted until the end of February 1940.

I left my bed during the most difficult period of that first winter. The house was cold. In the dining room was a little stove with its pipe hanging out of the window; we huddled around it warming our hands and "fronts", our backs ice-cold. Earning a living was becoming more and more difficult. Mamma started working in the place where her old primary school had been (the high school had burnt down). She set up a "children's kitchen" where teachers tried to do at least a little teaching. I don't know if there was any money from this but every day Mamma brought home her "ration" soup in a tin can which had held pickles. We ate this, the three of us, and it made life easier. Stefan, who had his parents to think about – two old people, his father recovering from a brain haemorrhage – started to sell off the remainder of his father's stock: chemicals, aromatic oils and other substances needed in the production of food substitutes. He established contact, or rather continued to cooperate, with the Strojwas company, a fact which proved lucky for many.* He was helped by his brother, Mietek.

It was a bad and icy winter that first winter of the occupation in Warsaw. Dark streets, covered in snow and rubble. Ruins everywhere, bricks and slabs of plaster falling from houses that had burnt down. In the apartments, boards in place of broken windows. Despite food supplies from the country, hunger was beginning to stare people in the face because money had lost its value and you had to barter for

* The Strojwas company, which made powdered soups, bouillons, etc., had a licence to operate during the German occupation, and was a source of employment for "outworkers" from the ghetto. Before the war, Mr Strojwas had been rather anti-semitic, but during the war he helped many Jews who knew him. (Author's note.)

food. And danger threatened. First news of the persecution of Jews, first incidents of assault in the streets, violent kicking as retaliation for not stepping aside fast enough, first shootings at defenceless people in the streets. News whispered from ear to ear, initially full of hope. Then, particularly after the fall of Paris, there was greater and greater hopelessness and fear. But we young people refused to lose heart. We believed that, despite everything, victory had to be ours. As long as we could hold out. "Until spring." We had to do something. Mietek quickly got a job in the children's hospital on Czysta street and began to urge me to try for a position as a junior house doctor in the same hospital for adults. But I dreamt of being a paediatrician. Dr Klemensia, our school doctor, came to my assistance. Her daughter was working as a nurse trained at the Bersohn and Bauman Hospital.

"Do you want to work there?" she asked me.

"Very much" I said.

PART ONE
❖ ❖ ❖ ❖ ❖

Superhuman Medicine

The Bersohn and Bauman Hospital

AROUND THE CHIMNEY STOVE

The flame burns in the chimney stove
And it is warm in the house.
The Rabbi teaches little boys
The alphabet.
Look children, remember, my loved ones,
What he's teaching you
Repeat it again and again
*Kumets, alef, u**
Study, children, don't be afraid
Every beginning is hard
Happy is he who learns the Torah
What more does a man need?
One day, children, you will be older
Then you will understand
How many tears there are in these letters
And how much despair.

YIDDISH FOLKSONG

* Letters of the Hebraic alphabet.

Chapter One

❖ ❖ ❖ ❖ ❖

THE HOSPITAL ON
SIENNA STREET

On 11 March 1940, I presented myself to the Head Doctor, Dr Anna Braude-Heller, at the Bersohn and Bauman Hospital in Warsaw on Sienna street. I already knew her a little, this short, black-haired lady who spoke in a deep alto voice and moved with surprising agility considering her weight.

She was the mother of a close friend of mine from the same study group at university, Arik Heller,* and the mother-in-law of a close childhood friend, Marysia Natanblut. But, in spite of this, my heart was in my mouth when I walked into her office.

The Head Doctor epitomized all the dreams and fantasies of a young student trained as a paediatrician. She was a well-known and respected doctor, a wonderful organizer and social worker. Apart from that, she was – a fact not without importance for a girl with her "head in the clouds" – a romantic figure. Always in deep black. After the death of her son from – what irony! – undiagnosed appendicitis, she never cast off her mourning. Later, when I had been working at the hospital for a while, she told me that this had been her greatest sin against Arik whom she'd deprived of the joys and light-heartedness of childhood. But that was later. That day, she looked over her glasses at the frightened girl before her and just said: "You want to work for us – fine. I'm assigning you to the ward for internal diseases as assistant to Dr

* Students in the Department of Medicine at the University of Warsaw were divided alphabetically into groups of 20–25. The author would at that time have been known by her maiden name, Adina Hertzberg-Szwajger.

Keilson. But first, please go and report to Dr Skonieczny. The next office along."

I thanked her politely. When I was at the door, she said, in a completely different tone of voice: "And Arik and Marysia haven't come back . . ."

I turned round and said on my way out: "I know they'll be back soon, doctor."

It was true. They came back after two weeks, Marysia in an advanced state of pregnancy.

In Dr Skonieczny's office, a slim, middle-aged man looked up at me from over his glasses and asked in a terrible Polish accent: "So, young lady, you vant to vork here, do you? As a trainee nurse?"

Well, I did look eighteen. Blushing to my roots, I replied: "No, sir. I've studied medicine and have come as an intern on the Ward for Internal Diseases."

"Vell, dat's gut. Please report to the vard."

"Thank you."

I left the office thinking – that German's not too bad. Dr Wacek Skonieczny! In all those dreadful years, when you were a friend to us, we never looked back on that first meeting.

The late Dr Waclaw Skonieczny was a Pole brought up and educated in Germany. It was probably thanks to his flawless command of the German language that he was appointed Dean.* I don't know. Maybe he had signed the *Volksliste*?† I don't know that either. But I do know that in the history of the hospital on Sienna street, there was his own beautiful chapter: "The Dean's Chapter". Not only did he not make it hard for us, he did all he could to help. But, for the time being, I had begun to play my own small part in the history of "superhuman" medicine, in the history of the children's hospital in the Warsaw ghetto.

I don't remember who took me up to the second floor

---

* The director of the hospital appointed by the Germans.

† *Volksliste*: the list signed by people of German origin (*Volksdeutsche*), who, though not full German citizens (*Reichsdeutsche*), declared their allegiance to the Third Reich and were granted additional rights.

through that unforgettable entrance hall with its semi-circular staircase winding in both directions. (When, after the war, this same building was being opened as the Hospital for the Children of Warsaw, I met one of our doctors, Dr Kachane-Kochanska, at the foot of these stairs, and we both just stood there for a long time, silent, helpless in the face of memories.) It was probably Jozio Ferszt – the administrator. At any rate, I was given two gowns to put on, one buttoning up at the front, and, to be worn on top of that, another buttoning up at the back; I was given a cap and a mask – such were the requirements – and I entered the ward. At that time, on 11 March 1940, this was an ordinary, proper ward, with glass-partitioned rooms so that the nurses could see what was going on, white beds standing against white walls and practically normal children with ordinary diseases. This was, after all, before the closure of the ghetto and these children were falling sick with ordinary children's diseases. Only it was, perhaps, a little more crowded than it should have been and it was a bit more difficult to get food. Yet infants were getting their usual mixtures – Nos. 1, 2, 3, 4 acidified (that's what they were called then) and "Dobo". And those who needed better nourishment were even getting extra eggs and cocoa! An ordinary hospital then, except perhaps even a little better than others because it was a hospital with a great tradition – a tradition of great Polish doctors, Dr Gantz, Dr Srebrny, Dr Simchowicz and many, many others – a hospital for all children regardless of their faith, truly a Hospital for the Children of Warsaw.

And that day, I met Hela Keilson with whom I wasn't to part company until that 22 April 1943, when we were all rounded up in our little café on Miodowa street and Marysia and I were left out in the street with no documents, money or anything else – above all, with no roof over our heads – while Hela and Marysia's sister, Halina, were taken to the Pawiak prison.* Halina broke down under the interrogations

* The Pawiak prison was set up and run by the Gestapo. Here Polish and Jewish prisoners were held, interrogated and tortured.

and admitted to being Jewish – she was shot. Hela, as Janina Malecka, held out to the end and was sent to Auschwitz. She survived the camp. After the liberation, she was taken to Sweden and never returned to Poland. I only received one letter from her – then she broke off all contact with us. Why? I don't know. But that was much later; I'll come back to that at the proper time.

But then, it was our first day working together and these were our first rounds. The head of the ward, Dr Lichtenbaum, was absent because of illness. Quite normally, Hela walked from bed to bed with Jurek Rotbalsam (the second assistant) and the ward nurse, to whom she was dictating instructions. For the first time in my life I was taking part in rounds no longer as a student but "performing the duties of a doctor".

I was given case histories to carry. I already knew I was going to be writing them up under the watchful eye of Hela – Dr Keilson to me at the time. I was happy; happy, proud and full of enthusiasm for what was opening up before me – treating children.

So, at the beginning, there was happiness.

But later, I delved into it all much deeper and happiness was replaced by helplessness and only this thought remained to the end: that we had our duty as human beings and that we were there to help. That is why this medicine was "superhuman" and why, although it is all like one great wound, it is the most beautiful thing of all.

Chapter Two

❖ ❖ ❖ ❖ ❖

FIRST MEETING

In the spring of 1940, there was an epidemic of meningitis. The treatment of it, at that time, consisted of serum administered straight into the cerebro-spinal fluid. I quickly became practised in helping with the punctures. My role was to fill the syringe quickly with serum (which, in fact, wasn't very easy), so as to have it ready just as the fluid was draining off, then take the test-tube with the fluid and place it in its stand. Considerable strength was needed to get a good grip on the child's head, with its stiff neck, and then to bend it back, so this was done by men. And one day the man in charge (I don't remember who) lost his grip on the child during the abrupt straightening movement and the needle broke between the vertebrae.

"Call the surgeons!"

The telephone was downstairs in the entrance hall, in the lab, in fact. I don't know how I managed to race down from the second floor but I do know that I jumped over the last banister from the height of half a floor and stormed into the lab.

"Call Ops! A needle's broken in the spine!"

Without an "excuse me", without a "good morning", without introducing myself to this tiny, beautiful woman in a white gown who, as I used to say later, didn't have her name tattooed on her forehead. But Dr Tosia Goliborska-Golobowa, the director of the lab, the owner of the lab on Kredytowa street, physician to the president, and a great lady, was terribly indignant at the "bad manners of the girl" who burst into her kingdom like a madwoman. Nevertheless she did as I asked.

Such was the disastrous start to my acquaintance with Tosia, an acquaintance which turned into a great and beautiful friendship which survived the war but didn't survive postwar days. Tosia, who had been warm and kind while in Poland in the sixties, was mortally offended that I didn't manage to send her the clay vase she'd bought here. Unfortunately, it broke while I was packing it. She didn't let me make amends and doesn't even know that my attitude to her hasn't changed, that my memory of her, now living somewhere in Australia, is that of a woman who so beautifully "set the tone" for the hospital and helped us always to live up to our humanity; that I have never forgotten and never will forget that on that terrible day, 30 July 1942, when I knew for certain that my mother, whom they'd taken the day before, had been deported, Tosia took the risk of coming to the ghetto for that one day in order to be with me. And on that day, as we were looking out of the hospital window that faced on to Zelazna street at the tragic procession of people being led out to the *Umschlagplatz** she stood beside me and held my hand.

But by then the hospital on Sienna street was no longer there. That whole little ghetto† over the bridge by Chlodna street was no longer there. It was the beginning of the end.

---

* *Umschlagplatz*: the square on Stawki street, next to the railway station, which had been used in the past as a loading depot. The Jews from the ghetto were gathered in this square before being sent to Treblinka; some of them were killed on the spot.

† The ghetto was divided by Chlodna street into two parts: a larger northern part and a smaller, southern part, known as the little ghetto.

Chapter Three

❖ ❖ ❖ ❖ ❖

QUARANTINE

But for the present it's spring, 1940. We're still in that wonderful hospital where for everyone – from the Head Doctor down through all the doctors, nurses and the whole of administration, to the humblest of auxiliary nurses or orderlies – children came first. Initially, there were the "normally" ill, whom we sometimes didn't manage to save because, at that time, medicine was even more helpless than it is now. And later there were the grotesquely bloated little bodies, swollen from hunger, to which skinny arms and legs had been attached like sticks to a badly made puppet. These we sometimes managed to save with glucose and vitamin C, a little powdered milk, a few grams of margarine, the remaining drops of watered down milk. But those times, too, had not yet come. In the spring of 1940, there was even room for hope. Hope that we'd pull through – "because, after all, this has to come to an end some time" – and hope that we'd lead a life of which we wouldn't be ashamed.

My "entry" into the hospital (i.e. into the fabric of all that was to happen there) began with its closure by the German authorities on the pretext of an alleged outbreak of typhus in the building. The entire staff, as well as the patients, were locked up in the hospital in front of whose gates stood a "navy-blue policeman".* No one was allowed to enter or

* There were two main police forces in Warsaw: the *Schutzpolizei*, German gendarmes who wore greenish uniforms, and the *Policja Granatowa*, the Polish police under German control who wore navy-blue uniforms. There was also the *Judischer Ordnungsdienst* (literally, the Jewish Service to Maintain Order), the Jewish police force created by the Germans, which operated only within the ghetto.

25

leave. At night, we slept side by side in the great library hall on the ground floor, under the portraits of the hospital's founders, the Bersohns and the Baumans. We ate in the canteen, meals which consisted of a plateful of watery soup. We took baths in the washroom in the hall, the so-called "bath on the catafalque" (before the war, this had been the admissions room – the bath stood high up). And we became one family. That dreadful move of the German authorities – to close people off in quarantine, to separate them from families and home, to subject them to hunger and discomfort – brought the entire staff together to form a tightly knit unit which nothing would be able to tear apart.

And it was probably during this closure that our "group" was formed – a circle of close friends which drew into its fold so insignificant a person as a young intern. This group included both the Keilson sisters: Hela, the doctor, and Dola, the hospital matron and "heroic nurse", so called because she would personally watch over every serious case, regardless of how many hours she had worked. To others, she left only those patients who were on the way to recovery. Dola Keilson, shot in Otwock in 1943 for being just precisely that – a heroic nurse. Beautiful, authoritative, alluring with her copper hair tied into a bun, she abandoned her safe shelter on the "Aryan side" so as to look after her long-divorced ex-husband who was dying of tuberculosis. Some louse informed on her. She was taken to Gestapo headquarters in Otwock but held out to the end. When asked whether she knew that she had been looking after a Jew, she answered that she was a nurse and was looking after a sick man.

"And would you look after a German, too?"

"If he was human, yes."

Then there was Tosia Goliborska-Golobowa. Evicted from her apartment on Kredytowa street, which had been turned into a German district, she now lived in the room next to the lab. Here, she collected what remained of her Meissen china, crystal glass and rugs. It was she who "directed" us in such a way as to make sure we wouldn't dare to lower our standards.

The only lab worker was Fecia Fersztowna, the administrator's sister, a woman from a pious and poor background, with a plain face and heart of gold, a wonderful friend.

Marek Edelman belonged to this group. At that time, he was the hospital runner and already brimming over with odd ideas and seemingly childish frivolity. And I myself, basically the same, probably included precisely because of my bubbling imagination and readiness for practical jokes or maybe because, for a long time yet, I wasn't to know fear.

Later, Dr Margolis – who, after the death of her husband, who was shot in Lodz, had come to Warsaw with her children to find shelter – joined this "select group". I don't remember when the hospital secretary, Bronka Feinmesser (Marysia), joined us. But it was after the "closure", which lasted a few weeks.

From time to time, guests – Jozio Ferszt, Dr Leneman and the charming Dr Kachane-Kochanska (she died of natural causes after the war) – were invited to the communal breakfast at ten o'clock in the lab. And these "breakfasts", our basic meal of the day, served on Meissen china and "drunk" from crystal glasses, consisted of one hundred grams of rationed bread, cut into wafer-thin slices, and ten grams of beet marmalade or five grams of "monkey lard". This was followed by one – literally one – twenty-five-gram glass of pure, undiluted *spirits* which we drank in one neat gulp. This one glass didn't make us tipsy but it did help us to work. We only discovered its calorific value later, during periods of extreme hunger when none of our group was swollen. Two hundred extra calories certainly proved vital. And after the closure of the ghetto, spirits were our only salvation. With a superb lack of consistency, the invader, while depriving us of food, provided doctors with spirit rations.

Chapter Four

✧ ✧ ✧ ✧ ✧

EVERYDAY LIFE IN
THE HOSPITAL

Closure of the ghetto was rapidly drawing near.* The appearance of the streets was changing – so was the hospital. Jews transported from other cities and towns were pouring into Warsaw. On the streets, there were more and more starved, ragged paupers begging for a crust of bread. In the hospital, more and more flea-ridden, lice-infested, fungus-diseased children. More children emaciated from hunger with the eyes of adults; more and more tuberculosis.

The TB Ward – a few small rooms on the third floor for children for whom there was no more hope. Children didn't recover from TB in those days. The head of this ward was Dr Margolis who, like the Head Doctor, believed that work should go on as usual, like it did before the war, that the sacred routine of a doctor's duties should not change an iota. In the mornings – treatments, blood tests, rounds, writing up instructions, then updating the case histories in such clinical order that they could be referred to years hence. The thought that these records might not be useful to anyone wasn't even allowed to cross our minds – nor the thought that anything regarding a sick child could be neglected.

The hospital day always began with a "report" – a briefing in the Head Doctor's office during which we not only discussed new or difficult cases but also had to *account for* every death and prove that everything possible had been done to save the patient's life. And there were more and more of these justifications . . .

* The ghetto was closed in November 1940.

28

The first such "collective death" was the death, within the space of barely a couple of weeks, of babies brought in from the Foundlings Hospital. The babies, emaciated with hunger, died of a "gluteal infection" which struck them down one by one. No treatment or medication helped; nor did special nourishment or dressings of the trophic skin changes. They all died quickly, practically without crying.

Then deaths on the TB Ward began. Children spent a long time there and weren't allowed to go out into the garden in case they infected others. They were strange children. Mature in their knowledge of the inevitable, yet at the same time cut off from the everyday atrocities of the ghetto as if by an invisible wall. Children who read wise books and discussed "life" but not "war life". A few were from the Korczak Orphanage,* among them Ariel, beautiful thirteen-year-old Ariel, who played the violin. There was also Zosia, a year older than him. And there was their love. The love of two children or, perhaps, the love of two adults whose entire life from childhood to maturity had passed in the space of a single wartime year on the TB Ward of the Children's Hospital. I made friends with those children. Every day, after three o'clock, I'd go to their ward and we'd talk for a long time and read books. Later, when I caught scarlet fever and spent six weeks on the ward for infectious diseases next to the TB ward, during the last two weeks when I was no longer "infectious", I helped them arrange an "artistic evening". Ariel played the violin and tiny six-year-old Ryfka danced the dance of the dying butterfly. She was as slender and beautiful as a butterfly and so liked to dress up in colourful ribbons and beads that we called her the "Hottentot". How joyously she laughed, dressed in her crepe skirts with colourful

* Janusz Korczak (pseudonym of Dr Henryk Goldszmid): doctor, writer and educator, who before the war founded an orphanage which was later enclosed within the ghetto. Offered the chance of staying behind in the ghetto during the deportations, he chose to go to the *Umschlagplatz* with his children. Diaries describe the orderly procession of children he led out of the ghetto. (See p. 50.)

streamers, and her wings of wire covered in paper flowers.

And like a butterfly, a few weeks later, she fell asleep in her little bed, never to wake up. Then later, on my birthday, on the first day of spring 1941, Ariel died. He had a difficult death, coughing painfully and choking on blood. We gave him morphine. And I, on the day of my twenty-fourth birthday, was given a present which was extraordinary in the ghetto – three freshly cut daffodils.

Ariel was in the hospital morgue. I went to him and laid down those three flowers. I had nothing else to give. My arms were empty and there were no words with which to say goodbye to a child who should have lived.

I was a coward that day. I didn't go up to the TB ward. I couldn't look Zosia in the eyes, Zosia who in her short life had already known love and death. I couldn't look at the empty bed of a child who had been as close to me as if he had been my own.

And as I was walking to the hospital gate, aware of my cowardice, I heard someone calling. The children from the TB Ward had seen me through the window. I went upstairs and heard: "Doctor, we know why you didn't come to see us. But don't be frightened. We're not in despair. After all, the same's going to happen to us."

The following day, we discussed Ariel's death during the "report". But this time we no longer had to account for it. We already knew that there was less and less we could do to save lives; that instead we were becoming, more and more, bestowers of quiet death. In search of the mercy of such quiet death, one cold autumn day, a ragged and homeless child stripped naked in front of the hospital gates and howled like a wounded puppy to be taken in because he was alone, hungry and cold. And when I was leaving the hospital one evening, I stepped on something soft: a baby's corpse, swollen, covered with newspapers.

Hungry children – there were more and more of them on the Ward for Internal Diseases, until finally they took up all the beds.

Every morning, we did the rounds of rooms which were still white but of a whiteness which had become the pallor of death. Every morning, we looked at the distended, deformed bodies, at the expressionless faces, and, with the same horror, we read the ages of those ageless creatures: four, five, six, sometimes ten or twelve. Cavernous eyes stared back at us, eyes so terribly serious and so sad that they seemed to be expressing all the sorrow of two thousand years of Diaspora. Hands lay motionless on the coverlets, children's tiny hands with bitten fingernails, tanned or pale, those same hands which only a few months back a mother had lovingly kissed and caressed. Children's hands, always lively and joyful, now powerless and subdued.

No, it's not true. No one gave in to despair: not the orderlies, who moved around with difficulty on swollen legs (after all, starvation didn't spare them either), nor the nurses, who worked ten to twelve hours regardless of their schedules. We, the doctors, also made our way, carrying not only the meagre medicines which we injected intravenously into swollen arms, but also the equally meagre rations provided by Joint:* half a powdered egg, ten grams of margarine – treasures which we couldn't entrust to the orderlies, who were dying of hunger, not because they weren't honest but because we couldn't expose them to the tortures of temptation.

Hunger is a terrible thing. And this was real hunger, the kind that kills. In 1964, invited by friends to an exhibition of photographs from the ghetto held at the IWO (YIVO),† I found a photograph of our hospital ward with Hela Keilson and Sabina, whose last name I don't remember. All I know is that with superhuman strength she would stand on her swollen legs and lift those heavy, helpless bodies, wash and

* Joint (the Joint Distribution Committee): the American organization which sent funds to the Jewish Self-Help Organization (later called the Jewish Organization for Social Care) – an international Jewish charity.

† IWO (YIVO): Institute for Jewish Research, New York.

change them and give them clean nappies until, one day, she didn't come to work. Struck down by starvation, she lay on a squalid bunk and waited for death. We managed to save her then. Every day, after work at the hospital, we'd split among ourselves visits to staff who were dying of hunger. We brought them the only thing we had – intravenous glucose, which sometimes restored their strength for a short while.

On such an occasion I caught typhus. I had gone to a displaced persons' camp* to give an injection of glucose and vitamin C to one of our orderlies who was lying in bed swollen from starvation. I sat down, in the dark room, on a low bunk by the window. Other people were lying there, side by side, but none of them was running a fever. When I left, I realized that I had "sat" on a nest of lice. They were crawling all over the blue dress with black stripes which I had put on that day, 26 June 1941, because it was the nameday of Zosia's husband, Wladyslaw. She celebrated this nameday, which was also their wedding anniversary, as if she could spirit him back in this way. (He was killed at Katyn.) And I went straight from this party to catch typhus.

Immediate delousing in the delousing chamber didn't help. On 13 July, I found I was feeling out of sorts and had a temperature of 38.8°C (102°F). It was a Sunday and I was the only one on duty on the typhoid ward. So I left home and went to see Maria Forman, a colleague from that ward – there were three of us there at that time for one hundred and fifty children – and I warned her that I might not last out my hours of duty.

I did my rounds and began to fill out the discharge forms and transfers from so-called *Verdacht* to *Sicher†* – this was a daily report for the German authorities which Marek, having

* Jews who had been driven into Warsaw were held in so-called displaced persons' camps.
† *Verdacht* – suspected. *Sicher* – certain.

a pass, took to *Stadtsartz* Schremf* early each morning. I remember that out of thirty forms I completed twenty-eight and stopped. I couldn't do any more. So I went to the Head Doctor's office and told her I had typhus and was going home.

She looked at me in horror with those black eyes of hers. "Go," she said. I took a rickshaw.† On the way, the driver ran into a German car. The German leapt out and started flogging him with his whip. I jumped out and went the rest of the way by foot. I spent two weeks at home in bed with typhus alone until midday because everyone went to work.

In the afternoons, colleagues from the hospital would come and give me injections of intravenous glucose, some kind of tonic and things to drink because thirst was the only thing pestering me, and again I'd lie in the haze of a 40°C (104°F) fever. The crisis came after fourteen days. The temperature suddenly dropped and I got up, dressed and went out into the street. No, I didn't collapse, I didn't die. I bought a quarter pound of cherries from a stall, went back home, put them on a plate and got back into bed. When Hela came that afternoon, she asked where the cherries had come from.

"I bought them."

"What do you mean, you bought them?"

"I just bought them downstairs."

Horrified, they worked out a duty roster. It had been a tiny, brief hallucination brought on by typhus, which passed in three days.

After three weeks I went back to the hospital. I spent the first week in a deckchair in the hospital garden, then simply went back to work. Back to the typhoid ward where children weren't dying. Except there weren't enough beds for them

---

* *Stadtsartz* Schrempf, the director of the German-run Department of Health for Warsaw, was known for his sadistic tendencies, brutality and extreme hatred of Poles and Jews. He worked closely with the Gestapo.

† "A rickshaw" was a vehicle built around a bicycle and used as a taxi in the ghetto (see illustrations between pp. 74 and 75).

and they lay two and sometimes even three to a bed, with little numbered plasters stuck to their foreheads. They ran a fever and kept calling out for something to drink. No, they didn't die of typhus. We discharged them but we were terribly tired because every day we took in a dozen new children and the same number had to be discharged or transferred from "suspected" to "certain" and the records of the typhoid ward were, after all, under German supervision. We discharged them so that they could die of hunger at home or come back, swollen, for the mercy of a quiet death. Such was each day.

Chapter Five

❖ ❖ ❖ ❖ ❖

CHILDREN I REMEMBER
FROM SLISKA STREET

Abram Federman had a "strange disease". He was losing the power of his arms and legs, which were subject to contractures. A neurologist came regularly to see him but there was nothing he could do. And Abram howled. He howled from pain and helplessness and his continuous screams were unbearable. Until somebody hit on the idea of putting a pencil between his contracted fingers and giving him a piece of paper. And Abram calmed down. Not only did he calm down. He smiled. And later he got some crayons too. He drew. He drew from imagination, from memory and from what he saw. And, one day, in one of those pictures, we saw a German gendarme who was giving a child . . . sweets.

Rafal Wichels, three years old, probably from the Foundlings Hospital, had been brought in with pneumonia during the "good days". Chubby-faced and mischievous, he laughed with the true laugh of a child. He'd endearingly cuddle up to our knees and say: "Give me chew-chews." He played with anything that fell into his mischievous little hands. He died of TB. His "pneumonia" turned out to be tuberculosis.

Aron, whose last name I don't remember, was the son of a rabbi. His head was so full of lice when he came to the hospital that it looked grey. It was only when you came up close that you could see that the grey mop of hair was moving. He felt the loss of his side-curls acutely when they shaved him bald in "dirty admissions". He cried and was frightened of his father. But the old rabbi who came to the hospital merely said: "How could we take care of the child when we

35

spent a week being herded and now there are fifty of us in one room. God will forgive you, my son."

Aron couldn't speak Polish. I made myself understood with difficulty using the few paltry Yiddish phrases I'd picked up from the children so as to be able to talk to them.

And Aron, grateful for every smile, for every word, tried to teach me a song his mother used to sing to him. And one evening, when I was sitting in the duty-room writing up the case notes, I heard the children talking about us and not about us.

"But they don't understand anything. What's the use of telling them about it."

"They don't know what it's like not having anything left to sell or eat, and that it hurts so much."

"Oh, when my sister died, Papa said it didn't matter where they buried her because we wouldn't live to visit her grave anyway. And Papa wrapped her up in paper and took her out into the street, but Mamma cried and wanted to snatch her away but she wasn't strong enough."

"I snatched a bit of bread from some people and they caught me and beat me. I don't remember what happened after that."

The ghetto streets were full of such "snatchers". Next to beggars, little paupers singing "Because we're young", these children who snatched parcels of food from passers-by or broke pieces off a loaf they were carrying were probably the hungriest of all.

Once, on Leszno street, a little pauper snatched a bunch of violets from my hand and ate it.

All the children admitted into the hospital had to have a blood sample taken for the Vidal test,* the Weil Felix reaction.† This even included those who, from the start, were condemned to die of tubercular meningitis which was still incurable at the time.

---

* Vidal reaction: test for typhoid fever and salmonella.
† Weil Felix reaction: test for typhus.

The task wasn't easy. It was hard to find a vein in those swollen or wasted hands. I learnt how to take blood from the zygomatic vein in the neck. That's why all the newly admitted children passed through my hands. And that's probably also why I was given the honour of taking blood from starving children for Tosia Goliborska who belonged to a group studying malnutrition.

I'd bring her the blood in tiny test-tubes and sometimes she'd tell us about the meetings of the research group.

Doctors in the ghetto not only continued to be doctors but, to the very last moment, kept up scientific research for those who were to follow.

The last research meeting of the group studying starvation took place in August 1942, when the round-ups had already begun. Dr Milejkowski* informed the gathering that this was to be their last session and instructed them as to where copies of their work would be hidden. The cemetery was one such place. A week after this meeting, practically nobody who had taken part in it was alive.

This wasn't the only research carried out by doctors in the hospital. Right up to the last months, within the hospital walls, scientific meetings would take place every fortnight where interesting cases (there were fewer and fewer) were discussed, as well as methods of treatment and there were even short lectures on theory. Twice a week, the Head Doctor would do her rounds of every ward – ordinary, prewar rounds, stopping at each bed and discussing every case in turn. One day, we were waiting on the ward, ready for the rounds. The door opened, the Head Doctor walked in and behind her, holding a gun at her back, was Schremf followed by two Gestapo men. Quickly, without a word, they passed through the ward. We stood there. But that time it ended there.

That day Felutka died. It was sometime in the autumn of 1941. She had already been on the surgical ward for six

* Dr Milejkowski: the director of the "Health Department" of the *Judenrat*.

months, was now three and everybody's favourite. "Give me the lecklace, I luf you," she'd say. Beautiful and full of fun, like somebody from a vanished world, she was a joy to behold. She had pleural empyema.* Repeated draining of the lungs proved useless. The surgeon decided to operate and the child died on the operating table. I'd left the TB ward on the third floor and was just on my way down when someone grabbed my arm and tugged me to the stairs with all her might. It was the Head Doctor. With a thundering voice, she shouted: "He's no doctor, he's a butcher! There's no place for him in our hospital! He killed the child." Her voice broke. I looked at her – tears were streaming down our director's face. Without letting go of my arm, she ran all the way down and when we finally reached the ground floor she let go of me and burst into the matron's office. In the middle of this hell of raging death, Anna Braude-Heller, the Head Doctor, was crying over this one death which could have been avoided. The hospital was her home; the sick, dying children, her children. She died with every child that couldn't be saved and constantly organized the devastated hospital anew.

The Head Doctor never left the ghetto. In the last letter we got from her, in March 1943 (three months after I had left the ghetto), she wrote: "Don't worry about me. I've got other plans" – and she remained among the rubble of the hospital on Gesia street, the last shelter for sick children. When the Hospital for the Children of Warsaw was opened after the war in its renovated building on Sienna street, it was not named after her. We were told that the times were not yet right for naming a hospital after Dr Anna Braude-Heller.

* Pleural empyema: a collection of pus in the cavity of the pleura.

Chapter Six

❖ ❖ ❖ ❖ ❖

THE HOSPITAL ON
LESZNO STREET

It was already autumn 1941. There seemed to be nothing left except helplessness. There were now not two, but three, even four children to a bed. If a child happened to get better, there was often no longer anybody left to collect it from the hospital. The working day was getting longer and longer, the nurses more and more tired as, staggering, they tended bedsores, laid the swollen bodies on their sides, "administered medication". Food shortages were becoming more frequent – even starvation rations were affected. One day, on the "older children's" ward, the famished skeletons threw themselves at the soup pot, overturned it as they pushed the nurse away, then lapped up the spilt slops from the floor, tearing bits of rotten swede away from each other.

Our "traditional" glass of pure spirits was no longer a symbol of past times; it had become an anaesthetic which enabled us to contort our faces into smiles as we made our way among the children.

But the hospital routine didn't change. The Head Doctor stood firmly by her principles: report, rounds, case histories which more and more frequently – nearly always – ended with the words: "died at . . . o'clock".

I don't know how much strength and courage it took to decide on opening a branch of the Children's Hospital. I don't remember the actual process of trying to find a building for it but I do know that some time in September or October 1941, we found out that some of the staff were to be transferred to the school house at the corner of Leszno and Zelazna streets. It was a sad, three-storey building right next to the

39

Wach, the gate in the ghetto wall. On the other side of Zelazna street, linked to the ghetto by a bridge, were the *Arbeitsamt** and the quarantine building for those who had been exposed to typhus.

There were three wards in the new hospital.

On the first floor was the Ward for Infectious Diseases, supervised by Dr Makower; on the second was Dr Hela Keilson's Ward for Internal Diseases; and on the third was the infants' ward, supervised by Professor Hanna Hirszfeld.

The Hirszfelds, because of their ostentatious conversion to the Catholic church, weren't popular in the ghetto. Despite all the respect that surrounded their scientific achievements, there was some sort of barrier between them and us. It was obvious that they considered it an additional injustice to have lost their position in the "better part of society". That's why the Head Doctor hesitated in employing Professor Hirszfeld. But, in the end, esteem for her as a really outstanding paediatrician prevailed, as did a feeling of human compassion for a mother helplessly looking on as her only child was dying.

Marysia Hirszfeld was dying of Simmonds† disease. I remember a research meeting or professor's lecture during which we looked in horror at this living skeleton of a young girl, adorned with jangling bracelets. And we looked at the face of the mother, holding her hand tightly.

Because there weren't enough posts at the hospital on Leszno street and Hela Keilson and I wanted to stay together, the Head Doctor officially appointed me as a delouser. This meant that, in addition to my normal duties on the ward, twice a day I had to check staff going in and out of work. Those who were found to have lice in their clothing had to go through the delousing chamber. This work, however unpleasant, was safe for me – I'd already had typhus and was completely indifferent to the sight of lice. They were

---

* *Abeitsamt*: Department of Employment.

† Simmonds disease: a failure of the pituitary gland, leading to weight loss.

simply a part of everyday life. However, I did have to take care not to be a carrier myself. But I was so hermetically dressed from head to toe in wellington boots, overalls, gloves and cap, that in all the time I worked there this never happened. Before going on to the ward, I'd have a bath and change "on the clean side" into ordinary hospital clothes. And so I was one of the most privileged people in the ghetto – a shower twice a day!

*   *   *

I don't remember the exact date we walked into that building and saw what was supposed to be a hospital. There were enormous rooms, no doubt old classrooms, built around the main hall – the same on every floor. And, in the hall, there was a long table with drawers where we wrote up our case notes. I don't even remember on what floor the doctors' duty-room was – probably the ground floor? I know it had a couch where you could sleep if duty permitted. And, in partitioned-off sections of the wards, there were also some duty-rooms, and cubicles for the nurses. On the ground floor, there was a huge room or rather huge hall which was later to be the "surgical station" where children shot by Germans at the *Wache* were brought. The way into the admissions room, the kitchen and the delousing chamber was through the garden, which wasn't a garden at all but an ordinary yard, and these rooms must have been in the basement. All this is very distant and hazy; only those hospital wards which we entered that October day in 1941 will remain in my memory forever, because neither before nor since have I seen anything like them, even though I've experienced the Warsaw Uprising and seen photographs of camp sick-rooms. The camp sick-rooms were even worse except that they had adults in them and adults have never moved me the way children do. Although now, now that I'm old and sick, I know that it's all exactly the same.

So there, in those enormous wards, on wooden bunks, on

paper mattresses with no sheets, lay children covered with the same paper mattresses. And in the corner of the room stood tin buckets because there weren't any bedpans or chamber pots and those children were suffering from *Durchfall* – the bloody diarrhoea of starvation – and couldn't get as far as the lavatory. So, in the morning, when you went in, those buckets were overflowing and slopping all over the floor – and there was a terrible stench of blood, pus and faeces.

On the bunks lay skeletons of children or swollen lumps. Only their eyes were alive. Until you've seen such eyes, the face of a starving child with its gaping black hole for a mouth and its wrinkled, parchment-like skin, you don't know what life can be like.

But we had white gowns and we weren't swollen because, after all, we did have our dose of spirits. So those eyes must have looked at us with hatred.

We weren't there to look at the horror, only to treat the sick or help with a quiet death. But, above all, to save lives because, even though times were bad, as bad as could be, we still wouldn't accept that it was of no use and thought that if we pulled through, we'd save those children and they would survive to the end. So we tried to save them with those scraps of food, medicines and injections and some of them got better. And when they began to get better, when, from those terrible, swollen lumps, skeletons began to emerge, we'd sometimes even see something resembling a smile. Except that this was the kind of smile that made your hair stand on end and your flesh crawl.

There weren't enough mattresses for the bunks and their number was diminishing because the bloody diarrhoea reduced them to pulp. The children started to get cold and cases of pneumonia broke out.

Then the Head Doctor decided to create a "matronage". Not a patronage, not a protective committee, but precisely a "matronage" – we were appealing to mothers. She told me to address the gathering, a gathering which consisted of all those in the ghetto who were still well off. (I remember that Gepner was there and Guzik, the representative of Joint, and many others.) I didn't quite know what to say to them, to the remaining few who were still well fed and well dressed. So I decided they'd have to be shown the truth and then things would develop of their own accord. I told them about the child who, in the frost, had stripped naked on the street in order to be taken in by the hospital because children came to us for that one last thing we could offer – the mercy of a quiet death. And I told them about little Ryfka who wanted to play and dance; and then I said that a little Rubinstein or Heine might be dying on one of those bunks. And that this hospital was a Golgotha where the little Jesus of the ghetto was falling under the weight of his cross – the Jewish child, thrice innocent, suffering a thousand tortures.

(I read all this a few years ago in the Polish edition of the *Folks-Sztyme*,* "translated from Yiddish" at that. I've no idea how or where the manuscript of this speech was found. But that, after all, isn't important. Except that the sentence about Golgotha and the Jesus of the ghetto had been left out – maybe it was blasphemy?)

We took them to a ward, only one I think, but that was enough.

In early spring, 1942, there were real beds in the wards, beds with real mattresses, and on these mattresses were white sheets and real blankets. There were even bedpans and chamber pots, mugs and bowls. So we were pleased. Really pleased. No doubt we didn't realize the terrible irony of those little white beds for children who in a few months time . . .

Meanwhile, despite these white beds and slightly larger food rations from Joint, medicine was becoming more and more helpless, because TB had broken out and prevailed all powerful. As soon as a child was able to get up and even begin to talk after the swelling from starvation had gone

* *Folks-Sztyme*: a Yiddish newspaper with a Polish supplement, distributed in Warsaw.

down, we'd do the Pirquet test.* The results were positive. And although there weren't any other symptoms of TB, we already knew that that child had only six to eight weeks left. So we didn't send those children to the TB Ward on Sliska street any more – there wasn't any point. Although, at the beginning, we did move them to different wards. For the sake of a clear conscience. But later on, even this was pointless.

Then we had the idea, like something from Grand-Guignol, of trying to put a smile on the faces of those children deprived of everything.

The Head Doctor's daughter-in-law, Marysia Natanblut-Heller, who had nothing to do because she'd graduated from the AWF,† came and in the afternoons the two of us tried to set up a "play room". Well, at the beginning, we just didn't know how to go about it. It was easier with the toddlers. When we'd gather them all in one ward or in the hall, they gladly listened to stories, even those about fairies, or they played . . . house. In the house, there'd be Mamma and Papa, and there'd be a table, and candles would be burning because it was Friday and on the table there'd be bread and "sprats". They'd make those stories up themselves – that there'd be bread and sprats. I never heard them make up anything about white rolls or Sabbath fish. And once they cooked soup for the children and there were "real" potatoes in it.

But we had absolutely no idea where to start with the older children because they were, after all, older and wiser than we by a whole century of suffering and by the deaths of those nearest to them. So, at the beginning, we told them to help us a bit with the little ones, those who wanted to, of course. Two or three of them came and the rest laughed at us – although we didn't see this. But one day, or rather one night, I was sitting in the hall on duty, filling out case histories by the light of a lamp, when I heard a conversation:

* Pirquet test: a skin reaction test for tuberculosis, now replaced by the Heaf or Mantoux tests.

† AWF: Academy of Physical Education, a Sports College.

"They're playing with the children . . . They think
that . . ."

"What?"

"Well, that this is ordinary life and that they're real children."

"Probably because they're still ignorant."

"Maybe they've never been hungry?"

"Or maybe they're scared and would rather be with us
than by themselves?"

"You know what? I'd actually like to be able to play and
walk around normally and sing. I liked singing."

"Sing something, Fajgele."

"What, in the middle of the night?"

"Tomorrow then?"

"Maybe."

"Let's tell stories."

"Well, when my sister died and Mamma carried her out,
she didn't have any strength left to go and beg, so she just
lay there and cried a bit. But I didn't have any strength to
go out either, so Mamma died too, and I wanted to live so
terribly much and I prayed like Papa did before, before
they killed him that is. He said: 'Shma Israel!' and I started
to say that too and they came to get the corpses and saw
that I was alive and they brought me here and I'm going to
live."

"Maybe we should say 'Shma Israel' too?"

I didn't hear any more because I dropped a file and the
children fell silent.

So the following day, when the older children came to
watch the little ones play house, I suddenly said: "Fajgele,
sing us something." "Why me?" "Because you look as if you
can sing." And Fajgele sang a lullaby. And then we started
to talk. Somehow it turned out that we were talking like
equals. That we were all equally afraid and that we, too,
didn't have much to eat but if we wanted to survive, we had
to try to live like human beings, we had to remain human
because they wanted to turn us into animals. I told them

45

how we learnt English on Sliska street. Then, finally, it somehow came naturally to tell them that they were young and ought to survive, that they mustn't forget that there used to be a time when they could smile. In the end, we all decided to organize a concert for Easter.

We organized the concert. Marysia (Natanblut-Heller) wrote a story for the children to act out – I don't remember what it was – and I enacted the song "Oyfn Pripechok"* with them. Fajgele was the rabbi; she sang, told the children to "copy her" and showed them the dance steps. The toddlers, dressed up as Heder† boys, danced a Hasidic dance. And there were some little cakes made from carrots or swede and artificial honey.

The children laughed and played, but I already knew that pretty Fajgele, Fajgele with her nightingale's voice, had a positive result for the Pirquet test, so it was only a matter of weeks. But I laughed so "merrily" that tears streamed down my face and the children shouted: "You're laughing so much you're crying." That was our last Easter, the Easter of 1942.

That same day, I was on duty at the gate, at the information desk. I'd sit there in the evenings and, while various doctors' wives accepted "parcels", I'd have records from all the wards in front of me and tell families about patients, how they were faring and whether they were still alive. Because these lice-ridden people in rags weren't allowed on the wards.

That very same day, six-year-old Ryfka came along. Her father was still at home but her elder brother and three-year-old sister were in the hospital. She no longer had a mother. The three-year-old sister died. "Ryfka," I remember saying, "take this parcel for your sister because she's dead now." And Ryfka looked up at me with those black cavernous eyes and said: "Because when a *person* has to do the washing, cleaning and cooking, she hasn't got time and I never managed to look after the child." And that "person", wrapped

* "Oyfn Pripechok" (Around the Chimney Stove): see p. 17.
† *Heder*: traditional Jewish school for boys.

46

in rags, turned and plodded away with the tired, shuffling step of an old woman.

I went to the ground floor to get my things and saw that there were people and white gowns in the hall. This meant that there were more wounded because "Frankenstein" was standing at the *Wache*.* He was a soldier who amused himself by shooting at children as if they were sparrows. When children came back to the ghetto after begging, they'd slip in through a hole in the wall one after another. He'd wait until there were a few of them, four or five "pieces" and then fire, dealing with them all in one go. But if a child was still moaning, we'd bring it to our hospital and Dr Wilk would come and have a look at it. Sometimes it was still possible to take the child to Sliska street for surgery but sometimes it was already pointless.

That same day, there was a little boy, maybe eight, maybe ten years old, who had been shot in the liver and there was nothing we could do to help him. Somehow I happened to stand next to him. Just then, he opened his eyes, looked at me and stretched out his hand in which he was clutching fifty groszy.† He said: "Give it to my mamma" – and died.

So that was my Easter evening on Leszno street. There was the concert and little Ryfka, who hadn't managed to take care of the child, and the boy whose life had been worth fifty groszy. I couldn't even give those fifty groszy to his mother because where was I supposed to look for her? I don't know what I did with them. After that, the end began to get closer and closer. But I still remember one more thing before the round-ups started and that is how Renia Frydman, who had gone to the same school as I had and who was working as an auxiliary nurse, came down with typhus and lay on the first floor on Dr Makower's ward. She was seriously ill and couldn't pass water for a couple of days. Then she had a dream that Hela Keilson, in the form of an angel, "had a pee

---

* *Wache*: one of the gates to the ghetto.
† The grosz was the smallest of Polish coins.

47

for her"; she woke up and passed water. After that it was
April and fifty-one people were shot dead. And 22 July 1942,
the beginning of the end, was rapidly approaching.*

That whole period is like one long night or one huge
shadow which enfolded everything and I can't remember
anything in sequence. There are only images that run into
each other – I know that's how things happened but what
and when? As if in a drugged stupor, we continued to keep
case notes although there was no longer any order to them,
because the hospital from Sliska street had joined us and we
were all together again. Except that there were fewer children
because the ones who were alive and who had parents still
had been taken away by them. But there was no longer any
hospital on Sliska street and there was no little ghetto. Tosia
Goliborska had already left the ghetto by then. And I don't
know how she managed to get to us that morning, the
morning following the night they took Mamma away, the
night I spent looking for help, the night Dr Makower, who
was a police doctor, came to the *Umschlag*† at five o'clock and
said that all the people who had been taken there the night
before had gone straight into the cattle trains. So I went to
work as usual and there was Tosia. Then we stood at the
window, or rather by the embrasure because they were firing
at the windows, and watched them being led away.

Dr Efros went by with her newborn son in her arms and
Dr Lichtenbaum, her mouth open as if in a silent scream;
and they kept going past, kept going past, with prams and
all sorts of strange objects, hats and coats and pots or bowls,
and they still kept going past.

Then suddenly Renia Frydman grabbed me by the arm
and shouted: "My parents! And Broneczka!" I said: "Don't
shout" because a gendarme had looked up in our direction.
And still they kept going past, those people. They kept going
past and it was a sweltering day, that 30 July, and silence

* The beginning of the deportations.
† *Umschlag*: abbreviation for *Umschlagplatz*.

hung in the air because there was no wind and the air was still.

A horse-drawn carriage rolled out from Leszno street – there, on the other side – and a young man in a blue shirt was sitting up in the driver's seat. He lit a cigarette and with a relaxed, sweeping movement threw away the match.

On the balcony of a house on Zelazna street – there, on the other side – a woman in a flowered housecoat was watering plants in window boxes. She must have seen the procession below, but she carried on watering her flowers.

And, on this side, they kept going past. They kept going past and there seemed to be no end. Old men with grey beards and little children and women in summer dresses and coats and women in raincoats, and bundles, all for that long trip ahead.

Sometimes, in my dreams, I see that carriage in the sun and that woman on the balcony.

I've no idea how that day ended but I think I remember saying goodbye to Tosia.

Afterwards, we continued coming to work in the hospital and often spent the night there because there were constant round-ups on the streets. And when they threw me out of my apartment because brushmakers* had moved in, I took my sheets and wrapped them round my records and Rosenthal china! I deposited all this in a little room on Leszno street which Stefan had somehow managed to procure for me and, when I went there three days later, it was all broken and jumbled up together, china and records, and the whole floor was covered with broken pieces inches deep; on top of all this, coumarin† had been spilt from the remainder of Stefan's stocks. But I didn't care any more. My pink nightdress was hanging on the door and I took that nightdress to the hospital with me. I put it on when I could take no more. No more.

* Jews working in German brushmaking factories within the ghetto walls.

† Coumarin: a white vanilla-scented crystalline ester, used in perfumes and flavourings and as an anti-coagulant.

And then we stood at the window again and watched Korczak and his children being led down Zelazna street towards Nowolipki. Apparently that was on 7 August, but I can't remember because we didn't keep track of the days.

We just kept walking among the children right up to the end, examining them and writing about them. And I remember how Dr Margolis praised me for keeping the case notes so well, but now I no longer know whether she was laughing or crying. And I can't ask her any more.

One day, I was finishing writing up case notes for Michal Jaszunski because he and his newly wed wife, Bronka, were dead – he had married her because his *Ausweis** apparently should have protected them both. I'd already written up case histories for him several times before because he hated doing it and said it was madness. But we thought that if those case histories were to survive, then, after the war, somebody would find them and there would be historical evidence.

And after that I hardly remember anything. Because the Germans came and took the children to the *Umschlag*. They moved the hospital and told the Head Doctor to reduce the number of staff. But I knew Arik was there with her and thought I wouldn't be affected; yet, at the same time, I thought it didn't matter to me anyway, now that they'd taken the children away. Except that I thought everything had to be left in order, so I sat down in the hall and finished writing up the records so that those who would go on to Stawki street would know what was what. Then I went to the duty-room and changed into my nightdress. That same pink nightdress which I'd taken from the burgled room on Leszno street. And I went to bed because I knew that nobody was going to be on duty here. There was only one phial of luminal† in the first-aid cabinet. That wouldn't be enough. But there was a bottle of vodka on the table, actually only a few dregs at the

* *Ausweis*: an identity card specifying a person's place of work; more generally any type of identity card in the Third Reich and Warthegau.
  † Luminal: sleeping tablets.

bottom. Half a glass. I poured the vodka into a glass and thought that together with the luminal it should be enough. I swallowed the luminal – ten tablets, that's how many there were in the phial – and drank the vodka in one gulp. I felt good. A bit sick but not very. I was already feeling sleepy. Then Hela Keilson came in. I hadn't fallen asleep yet and she asked: "What have you done?" because she'd seen the empty phial. I answered her that I'd completed all the case notes and filed them away and then she started screaming. There were more people in the duty-room by then and they held me firmly by the arm, straightening it so as to be able to stick a needle into the vein, but I cried: "Leave me alone! It's all over. There's no need." And then I felt a prick, heard a ringing and that's it, I can't remember any more. It was only later that I found out that Hela Keilson had put twice as much cardiamine as glucose into the syringe because she'd mixed up the ampoules, in her agitation, and I'd suffered a reaction to the cardiamine. So I don't remember anything more about the hospital on Leszno street.

It wasn't until thirty-seven years later, when I read what Marek had said, that I found out that he had been the one to carry me out in that pink nightdress.

Chapter Seven

❖ ❖ ❖ ❖

THE INHUMAN END OF
SUPERHUMAN MEDICINE

I woke up after a couple of days, perhaps more, in some unknown apartment. I can't remember who was there. I knew some of the people, others I was seeing for the first time. They told me that the hospital staff had made their quarters on Pawia street and that the Children's Hospital was on Stawki street, on the *Umschlagplatz*. The hospital, next to an out-patients' department, was located in one wing of the Polytechnic (Craft) School, while the other wing already formed part of the *Umschlag* where, when there was a shortage of cattle trucks, people would wait before being deported.

After a couple of days, I was taken to some apartment on Pawia street, and we were all together again. Dr Margolis, Hela Keilson, Marek, myself and a lot of other people. And every morning, dressed in our white gowns, we were led, as a group, to the hospital on Stawki street, to the *Umschlag*, and then back to Pawia street.

So I arrived at the apartment on Pawia street, and the hospital on the *Umschlag*, a little later than the others. But I was there for three weeks as it was. And every day, once the cattle trucks had left, I'd go to the deserted square and gather children who had been abandoned by their mothers. Maybe the mothers had wanted to save the children from death, or maybe only themselves? Fear of death is something that can't be described. You have to live through it to understand. I lived through it, too, but that was much later and an entirely different case. But at that time I didn't feel anything at all when I'd go out into the yard, show the Ukrainian soldier a bottle of vodka and drink some of it first; he'd finish the rest and I'd gather the children and take them back to the hospital.

Once he was talking to me when a little girl appeared at a window of the *Umschlag*. He raised his gun, shot her and carried on talking to me. I picked up a child, said goodbye to him and walked away – only I didn't know how to hold the child so that it wouldn't be hit if the Ukrainian shot at me. Later, the children who had been "saved" were sent to the ghetto by ambulance because the ambulance kept going to the end. And I don't know who picked them up there. Some of them came back to the *Umschlag*. But, what's the difference? They all died anyway. It's just that, at the time, I did think there was a difference.

And sometimes there were families.

In 1964, when I was on a visit in New York, Stasia told me that, when we left the hospital during the round-ups and got into the ambulance, I was pulling her in while the driver was pulling her out and I shouted: "You swine! I saved your child from the Square yesterday and you . . ." And he calmed down. So those children probably did have families.

And that's how it was to the very last day. I don't know what day it was. But I think it was 4 September, or maybe . . . No, it was a day or two earlier. Anyway, it was the day they brought all the patients from all the hospitals in the ghetto to the hospital on Stawki street, where the children had already been for a couple of weeks. What happened was that, when I woke up in the morning at "home" on Pawia street – because that was our "home" then – they told us that all the Jews from the ghetto were to assemble in the block between four streets – Mila street, Zamenhoff street, Gesia street and Smocza street – and that we, too, were to go there. And then Dr Margolis and I said we were going to the hospital. And somebody else went too, a few people, I can't remember who any more. All I know is that we went down empty streets and I don't even know whether Marek was with us then. I know that we were together later on but I don't know about that time. All I remember is that we were wearing our white gowns and I don't think they were shooting at us; but maybe they were? I don't know. I'm old now and I can't remember.

I only remember the hospital gates and those stairs strewn with people and that terrible stench of pus and faeces and that somebody was constantly grabbing at my gown and shouting: "Sister! Sister!" This was something quite different from hospitals during the Warsaw Uprising later on, although they, too, were terrible. Here, I know that I kept going up the stairs, trying not to step on people, but there – corpses and living all lay together. I reached our third floor and there was only the infants' ward – no children's wards, just the sick, the wounded and the dying everywhere. But, as I walked around, children began to appear from various nooks and crannies and gathered around me – like birds or puppies – and, as we walked on, more and more of them appeared until we reached some kind of ward and sat down. And then Marysia, who had tuberculosis of the lymphatic glands – called scrofula at the time – said to me: "Doctor, we all know that we haven't got mammas or papas any more and that we're not going to live through it either. But will you stay with us to the end?"

"Yes, Marysia, I'll stay with you to the end," I said.

This was only half true because I did leave but they were already asleep by then and weren't supposed to wake up. Yet sometimes, even now, when I can't sleep, I wonder whether any of them woke up. But it's better not to think about it.

At that point, I wasn't thinking about it yet and had no idea whether we'd get out of there alive. A whole day lay ahead of me. Hela Keilson was downstairs with a bandaged leg and, in the bed next to hers, was the head cook, swathed in bandages. Both were suffering from burns because a few days previously the head cook, proud that she had managed to cook some swede soup with carrots for the children, wanted to show it to Hela. Hela went down to see it and the cook was so pleased with her soup that, without looking behind, she sat right in the huge cauldron of soup which was already standing on the floor. What spluttered out scalded Hela Keilson's leg so that she couldn't walk for several days.

So I sat there with them, because the Germans and the Szaulis* had burst into the hospital looking for "foreigners" and Hela and the cook weren't lying in a ward but downstairs in a little room just off the duty-room. So when the Szaulis burst into the room, I was in the process of changing a dressing for the cook and they moved on – stating that everything was in order. And there, in the room next to ours, was Zosia Frakter, also a young doctor. She'd poisoned herself. She'd found out that they'd taken her mother away. All I remember is that when I was going back to the ward from the room where the two scalded women lay, somebody was carrying Zosia's corpse in his arms and, no doubt, she lies "buried" there somewhere. Maybe where the Inflancka street depot is today – I don't know.

Then I went back to the ward, to the room where the children were sitting, and Dr Margolis was there, too. The Head Doctor was in her office. I know we went to see her because I remember her saying that she didn't want to distribute the "life tickets".† I remember telling her: "If you don't, Doctor, then none of us is going to survive because the director of the adults' hospital is going to do it instead." Everybody said she had to do it but it was vile, because, after all, none of us would like to decide who is to live and who is to die, yet we demanded it of her. Heads of wards, apparently, were automatically allocated "tickets" but the fate of the rest had to be decided. Later on, after the war, I asked Arik Heller if he knew why it was us who got "tickets"; that is, people like myself and not the older ones who were a thousand times more valuable. He told me then that his mother had staked her bets on youth, that we might live through it all and still do something with our lives. And so it was that from our

* Szaulis: Lithuanians in the service of Germans.

† Cards with numbers on them, distributed to those who were "needed" and were to stay on in the ghetto.

group, Dr Margolis and her daughter, Hela Keilson, Marek and I were given permits; but not Stasia because she wasn't from our hospital – we had only taken her to Stawki street with us so as not to be separated. And Marysia and Dola Keilson must already have been on the Aryan side with Wacek Skonieczny. At any rate, I don't remember them there, at the *Umschlag*.

So, from the room where the two scalded women lay, I came back to the children and sat with them, because there was nothing else I could do except sit and talk to the children and tell them what it used to be like. Sometimes the conversation kept going, sometimes it petered out, so we sat in silence, those fifteen children and I. Then Sister Mira came for me – I can't remember her last name but I still see her face in front of me as if she were here now. And she asked me to go downstairs with her for a moment. When we left the ward, she said – and I can still hear this – "Doctor, please give my mother an injection. I can't do it. I beg you, please. I don't want them to shoot her in bed, and she can't walk."

So I asked her what was in the syringe and she told me it was morphine. I knew then what I could do for the children so as to keep my word. Although I didn't know yet that I had been given a "ticket", I did know we'd be separated and I wouldn't be able to help them in that final moment. I asked her if she had a lot of morphine – she said she'd give it to me. Because she knew what I wanted it for.

We went to the first floor where the families of staff were. (My father-in-law had been there but Mietek had taken him away. I would have helped him too.) And so that grey-haired lady smiled at me and stretched out her arm. The sister put on the clamp. And I injected the morphine into her vein.

And then I saw a few more people who didn't have the strength to move.

I asked Mira what we should do and she said: "Help them, surely." So we helped them, too. And by the window there was this woman, swollen from starvation and suffering from circulatory insufficiency, and she kept on looking at us, pleading with her eyes. She was the last one we gave an injection to.

And it was only later, much later, that I discovered that this was Dr Lendsberg's wife. And this "scene", when he found out about it from me, made its way into one of Rudnicki's short stories.* "Ascension", I think it was. Except it wasn't quite the way he describes it. But that doesn't matter . . . So when I left the room, I held out my hand and got two large containers of morphine. We didn't say a word to each other, just squeezed each other's hands, I think.

I took the morphine upstairs. Dr Margolis was there and I told her what I wanted to do. So we took a spoon and went to the infants' room. And just as, during those two years of real work in the hospital, I had bent down over the little beds, so now I poured this last medicine into those tiny mouths. Only Dr Margolis was with me. And downstairs, there was screaming because the Szaulis and the Germans were already there, taking the sick from the wards to the cattle trucks.

After that we went in to the older children and told them that this medicine was going to make their pain disappear. They believed us and drank the required amount from the glass. And then I told them to undress, get into bed and sleep. So they lay down and after a few minutes – I don't know how many – but the next time I went into that room, they were asleep. And then I don't know what happened after that. All I know is that I had my "ticket" pinned on me and that I took "tickets" to the scalded women. Hela Keilson got up, but the head cook had poisoned herself with luminal and we left her there. And then there was the hall downstairs in the hospital, just by the door, and people pushing to get out. I met one of my schoolteachers there, Dr

* Adolf Rudnicki: Polish writer and essayist. The story "Wniebowstapienie" was first published in the journal *Kuznica* (1948), and later in the collection *Ucieczka z Jasnej Polany* (1949). An English translation by H. S. Stevens was published under the title "Ascent to Heaven" (1951).

Stefania Zlotowska, and she asked me bitterly: "Have you got a ticket?" But I didn't know what to say because I was ashamed. I don't know how I managed to take half a litre of pure spirits with me in that confusion. All I know is that in all that pushing and shoving, I didn't let go of Hela and Stasia. And that was probably the worst thing of all – all those people with "tickets" pushing to get out and live, while all the others were left behind.

The fact that we got out alive, that we got out of that hell in the hospital hall, is important even now. I don't know if it's any excuse that we were so young and wanted to live. And, after being saved from that rehearsal for death, I really did want to live, even though I still didn't know what it was like to be truly afraid. And that's why we got out with those silly "life tickets" while others were left behind.

After the round-up, over a period of a couple of days, we kept sending our "tickets" back to the hospital to those who were left behind – but only left behind in the sense that they were the last to be taken away – and, in this way, a few people were saved. But that doesn't change anything. Nor does anything that happened afterwards. Another four months on Gesia street where there was a so-called children's ward and two years on the Aryan side. I'll write about them – those two whole years – but they still didn't manage to wipe out any of what had happened the day I gave the children morphine. Nor did they wipe out the escape. And that's why I was always different from everybody else. And nobody ever understood this. Everybody thought I'd forgotten about everything and didn't care any more. I'd hardly see anybody who came to visit. I didn't want to.

Chapter Eight

❖ ❖ ❖ ❖ ❖

REQUIEM FOR THE HOSPITAL

Do you remember – yes, it's you I'm asking, the only person who has remained here.* There's nobody else. Four hundred thousand were killed. The few – few score thousands – who were left are now scattered all over the world. So you're the only one I can ask: do you remember how the two of us walked down the street of that dead city?

Where were we going? And why? Don't you remember?

It was already after the round-up. We'd been led out of the trap and taken to 6 Gesia street. To a tenement block. That's where the hospital for the remaining forty to fifty thousand was to be. Three small rooms on the first floor, that was the children's ward. Just right for the couple of hundred children still alive. One annex was for staff apartments.

Our apartment was on the third floor. Three small rooms and a kitchen. There were a lot of us in those three rooms, ten to twelve people, I think. So, in the evenings, we'd put a pot of "mock cholent"† to simmer on the stove: a little buckwheat, potatoes – if there were any – and sometimes thirty grams of lard. And salt. In the mornings, we'd all pour ourselves a plateful of hot soup and go to the hospital, because we were still working there.

So why were we walking down that street? What were we looking for in that silence which screamed in our ears, in those yards where water dripped from standpipes and feathers swirled in broken windows? Why did we peer through

* The only person who has remained here: Marek Edelman.
† Cholent: a thick broth.

59

those windows into houses where photographs hung on the walls, a half-drunk glass of tea stood on the table and, on the floor, lay a wooden horse and tiny shoe?

Do you remember? Someone was shooting at us. He was sitting there somewhere, that German who had suddenly seen two silhouettes divested of human dimensions and had tried to blow them away. Only he kept missing, though the bullets whistled past our ears. But it didn't matter because we'd already experienced our own deaths. So we talked about how we were going to write about what had happened. And we did write something. Except that later, much later, there was the Warsaw Uprising and everything perished in the ruins of St Alexander's church.

Maybe we were looking for something we could chop up and burn in the stove, like that tenants' letterbox which we carried up to our third-floor apartment. Or maybe we were looking for something to eat. When we broke away from the round-up and came to this building, we did, after all, start by rummaging through the wardrobes and cupboards. And we found some tea, buckwheat and a bag of beans. All we thought about was how to cook that buckwheat as quickly as possible and eat. I don't know – I can't remember.

The Head Doctor was on the ward, and Hela Keilson, and I don't know who else.

I don't remember much from that ward. Even though I went to work there every morning. In the afternoons or nights, I worked as an orderly because there weren't any orderlies and we didn't need so many doctors.

I can't remember? No, that's not true. All I have to do is start thinking about it so as to bring back the smell, the stench of putrefying flesh. So as to see Chamele, who was ten and laughed with her entire thin face, saying she was so glad that nothing was hurting her. After all, you could live without toes and perfectly well at that. Except she kept apologizing that her legs smelt so much.

And Chaim asked us to save his fingers because he wanted

to play the violin like his papa who had been left behind in the snow and the mud on the road to Warsaw.

Was it cold, that winter of 1942–43? It must have been, because in the evenings human shapes would flit by in the streets wrapped in layer upon layer of rags. And the children, on their beds, shivered from the cold because there was a shortage of fuel and there's no warmth to be had from being thin.

But there weren't any swellings from starvation any more because, in that neighbourhood, we had the rations of those who were now nothing but smoke blowing across the fields of Treblinka.

So there was more bread, artificial honey, and from those who worked "the outposts"* we'd buy fifty grams of lard or half a pint of horse's blood.

Do you remember? We got bread from the brushmakers on Swietojerska street in exchange for the sugar and sausages which Dr Skonieczny had brought when he still had his pass. Except that we weren't very good at bartering, so we just stood in the yard and waited to see what would happen. It was my yard and I found photographs there.

So there were no more swellings from starvation although there wasn't that much to eat. There were only burns and frostbite.

But I wasn't working as an orderly any more because I'd cut myself while washing the floor in the typhus isolation ward where Stefan lay, and I had a horrible phlegmon.† I was in bed for ten days. Dr Wilk made an incision for me at home and then I became his assistant.

There was no more child surgery. So Dr Wilk was in charge of a "little surgery" for the whole hospital.

I don't know, I can't remember where I sterilized the instruments. There was a sterilizing vessel somewhere. All I

* Jews who were sent to work each day as "outworkers" on the Aryan side.
† Phlegmon: an inflammation, particularly of the cellular tissue, which tends to suppuration.

remember is following Dr Wilk around the wards with a tray covered with napkins. And I understood more and more clearly that you had to bring help right up to the very end, but first you had to be made of stone.

No, I don't dream about it any more. It's passed. Except that later, when I was working in the hospital during the Warsaw Uprising, I looked at everything through blind eyes. Because nothing could compare to bedsores all over the buttocks, dead tissue cut away with ordinary scissors and no anaesthetic. Or people who had been burned while working on the Aryan side, lying on sheets soaked in saline solution.

Frost-bitten feet were an everyday occurrence, fingers and toes black with gangrene, amputated on the bed without a table, even without gloves – we'd simply wash our hands. And the stench – the terrible stench.

I didn't like my children's ward then. I didn't like assisting during the amputations of tiny frost-bitten fingers or the bandaging of little children who had been fatally burned through lack of care. I didn't like it – that's all.

What I remember best from that period were the students from the nurses' school, still under the iron hand of Luba Blum-Bielicka, the school head – even in that last pre-burial home. Doing the rounds of the typhus wards at six o'clock in the morning, she'd ask, in her characteristic Wilno drawl: "Have you been washed today?"

One morning, a student, hurrying to get everything done before the school head's inspection, rubbed down, with spirits, the backs of dead people who had been put out into the corridor during the night.

And we kept walking around the wards, pretending to those who were dying that there was still hope.

Such was our hospital.

*   *   *

Then came the next round-ups. 18 January 1943.

We woke up, that January morning, and heard shouting

in German. One of the boys ran downstairs, came back and said that the round-ups had started.

So we had to get dressed and wait to see what would happen.

Suddenly there was a knock on the door and a Gestapo man came in. He looked as if he'd stepped out of a picture – there were such beautiful boys among them, only their eyes were made of ice. He looked everyone up and down, then came up to me.

"Who are you?"

"A doctor." I already had my gown on and a stethoscope around my neck.

"Are you afraid of dying?"

"No" – and that was true. Because I didn't feel anything.

And he drew out his gun, put it to my forehead and said something about not really wanting to but *"Befehl ist Befehl"*.*

But still I wasn't afraid. Only everybody else was frightened, because it wouldn't be very nice to have a corpse right there with its brains blown out and all that.

After a moment, he tossed the gun in his hand, smiled because his joke had worked and yelled at the men to go downstairs "to help the sick". So the boys rushed out of the apartment but hid somewhere, of course: in the gateway? In a hiding place?

And when he left, the problem of hiding ourselves arose. There was a hiding place on the second floor which some merchant must have made for his goods. It was a long, narrow passage which ran in the opposite direction to the rooms and the door to it was blocked by a wardrobe.

I had absolutely no intention of going in there, but it so happened that Hela's parents wouldn't go without her, and she wouldn't go without me. So Marek told me: "You've got to go. We've got guns and don't want the old people around in case there's shooting."

There were about thirty people in that "shelter" and the

* *Befehl ist Befehl*: Orders are orders.

candle which we lit went out after an hour because there wasn't enough oxygen. But before I sat down, I noticed a heavy – what must have been a two kilogram – weight on a shelf. I sat on the stove next to the shelf.

And then we heard them break down one door after another and when they entered our apartment, we heard a loud splintering noise as if they were pushing the wardrobe aside. That's the first time I felt cold, especially my legs. And that, precisely, was fear. But I grabbed the weight and can't remember if I was still frightened after that. Then we heard them saying: *"Ist nichts da"* and they went away.

It was a long time before anybody moved. Later on, it turned out that when they were opening the wardrobe they wrenched it so hard that the back fell out and covered the door to the hiding place.

Then we heard three shots. And there were three people left in our apartment. That was when I really knew I was afraid and shook as if I'd caught a chill. And when everything was over, the Head Doctor looked at me, waiting for me to go and see if it was safe to come out, but I couldn't because I was still shaking. And it was only when somebody came to get us and told us it was over that I took Fecia and went through their apartment and through some rubble over to ours. But everything was fine there. Only the sick were gone.

But times had changed. For three months now, the Jewish Fighting Organization had ruled the ghetto. Thoughts about myself were less important than thoughts about how to die. People were uniting, people who, in a few months time, were to go up in flames like some great firework visible to the whole world. During those January round-ups, shots had been fired from the other side, our side. Dead German soldiers lay in Jewish streets. On 18 January, Szlengel wrote the poem "Counterattack",* copies of which circulated throughout the ghetto within a matter of days. But for me, the second period of history had begun. On 25 January 1943, I went over to

* See p. 69.

the Aryan side. Marysia, who was already there, and I organized means for people to leave the ghetto. We prepared apartments, and documents for those who were able to move.

We took in the people closest to us, our colleagues from the hospital. The last person who managed to get over to us was Renia Frydman (Zosia). Then we wrote that letter to the Head Doctor begging her to leave because we had everything ready for her. We got the reply: "Don't worry about me. I've got my own plans." So, for a moment, we believed that, like many other eminent doctors, she had some other way out.

But there was only one way for her: together with the hospital.

And we don't really know how she died. Whether in the flames of the burning hospital, or somewhere in a cellar. Or maybe she was amongst those who were taken away. We don't know.

*   *   *

Two more years began. Years during which I got to know hate and fear. Fear, which turns hands and legs into blocks of ice. But that's an entirely different story.

*   *   *

Years have passed since then. Many years.

There's no trace, in this great, modern city, of what happened here. Yes, there is a monument.*

But not even a single fragment remains of the wall which separated one third of the residents from the rest; not a vestige of the stone desert which they made of the place where people lived, fought and died – people who had been there for a thousand years. Not a single burnt-down house from whose

* See illustration facing p. 75.

windows mothers had thrown their children and jumped after them.

Sometimes I walk through that new, modern neighbourhood, along pavements which cover the bones of those who were burnt there. I look up at the sky, there where my house and all the other houses once stood.

When I close my eyes, the streets become familiar again. A crowd of people – shadows – wander among the shadows of houses and, clearly, as if they were real, I hear the voices of children, crying in that other language: *"Hob rachmunes!"* Have mercy!

Sometimes I come to Sienna or Sliska street. I look at the hospital gate, peer through the railings and see that the Paradise apple trees that used to blossom there have gone. The hospital does not bear the name it should.

But I close my eyes. And the gate opens – the one on Sliska street where once a homeless child had stripped naked – and all the people who have disappeared pass through it.

There is the Head Doctor, in her white gown, doing her last rounds, and behind her the doctors, nurses and orderlies, then the administrators and Dr Kroszczor, who carefully closes the gate behind him.

I know that they've left everything as it should be and that Dola Keilson has swept all the floors.

PART TWO

❖ ❖ ❖ ❖ ❖

Counterattack

– ZOB (The Jewish Fighting Organization)

✧ ✧ ✧ ✧ ✧

COUNTERATTACK

18 January

Quietly, as if past caring, they went to the wagons,
Sullenly they looked the Szaulis in the eye – just cattle!
The officers were pleased that things went so smoothly,
That the stunned hordes kept marching,
And jauntily cracked their whips. At faces!
Silently the crowd collapsed in the square,
Holding their sobs for the wagons.
Their blood and tears soaked into the sand,
While the *Herrenvolk* casually threw the cigarette packets
    on their bodies –
*Warum sind Juno rund?**
Till that day when into the town lulled by propaganda
They came at dawn, like hyenas out of the morning mist,
and the meat woke and bared its fangs.
The first shot rang out in Mila street,
A gendarme staggered at the gate,
In disbelief, froze for a moment,
And cursed: "O hell! I'm bleeding!"
But already the Brownings were crackling
In Niska, Dzika and Pawia streets.
On the winding stairs, where an old woman was dragged
    down by her hair
Lay SS-man Handke.

---

  * *Warum sind Juno rund?* (Why are Junos round?): a common German cigarette advertisement of the period. Juno cigarettes were round, like today's cigarettes, at a time when most cigarettes were flat.

As if unable to take death, as if choking on the revolt,
He coughed up blood on to a packet – *Juno sind rund, rund,*
    rund.
And roundly is all being answered:
The gendarme in his blue uniform lies on the spit-stained
    stairs in Jewish Pawia street, unaware,
That at Szultz's and at Toebbens'*
Joyful bullets dance and sing.
The meat defiant, the meat insurgent, the meat fighting!
The meat spitting grenades from windows,
The meat spouting forth scarlet flames,
The meat clutching at the rim of life!
What joy to shoot between the eyes!
You are at the front now, *meine Herren!*
Hier trinkt man mehr kein Bier,
Hier hat man mehr Mut,
Blut, Blut, Blut.†
Now off with your nice soft leather gloves,
Now down with your whips and on with your helmets!
Here's our communiqué for tomorrow:
"We drove a wedge into Toebbens' block."
The meat defiant, the meat fighting, the meat in full song!
Hear, German God, thus Jews pray in their "den-like"
    dwellings:
Wielding an iron bar, or a club.
We beg you, O Lord, for a bloody battle,
Grant us, O Lord, a valiant end,
May our death shield us from the sight of unending rails.
O Lord, steady our hands,
Let them stain the blue uniform with blood,
Grant us, before we utter our last silent groan,
The sight of those arrogant hands, those hands wielding
    whips,

---

* Szultz and Toebbens: large German workshops in the ghetto.
  † *Hier trinkt man mehr kein Bier/Hier hat man mehr Mut/Blut, Blut, Blut:*
Here you don't drink beer any more/Here you need more courage/
Blood, blood, blood.

COUNTERATTACK

Trembling with commonplace, animal fear.
From Niska street, from Mila street, from Muranow
Our gun barrels flower with scarlet flames.
This is our Spring! Our Counterattack!
Like wine this battle goes to our heads!
These are our Partisan forests: the corners of Ostrowska
    and Mila streets,
On our chests shake our block-numbers –
The medals of our Jewish War.
The word revolt strikes like a battering ram,
And on the street a trampled packet lies, sticky with
    blood:

          Juno sind rund!

              WLADYSLAW SZLENGEL

Chapter Nine

❖ ❖ ❖ ❖ ❖

A COURIER GIRL FOR ZOB

It was just after the second wave of deportations to the camps, which took place on 18 January 1943, that it all began. We had a few more days together in our flat at 6 Gesia street. What little I can remember of them is grey and empty, like a piece of underexposed film. But I do remember. We used to go to work, and clean the empty wards from which our few dozen patients had been taken away in the lorries. We would sit at home and talk. Or just sit in silence. The boys, Marek Edelman and Welwl Rozowski, used to go out early in the morning. They were busy with their own affairs – that is, with ZOB. And we used to sit there trembling, not knowing whether they would return alive that evening, waiting for any news and any orders which they might bring. Orders telling us what we were to do in the future – for at that time there was still a "future". We were still alive.

"Tomorrow," said Marek, on the evening of 24 January, "you are going over to the Aryan side with the work party. Get yourself ready."

But I really didn't want to go. Playing the simpleton, I told him that I didn't have the money to pay the foreman of the work party. You had to pay to go with them, and it was very expensive. The foreman of the "work party" (which consisted of Jews going out to work on the Aryan side) used to smuggle out among the workers those who wanted to escape from the ghetto. He had to bribe the gendarmes at the gate, who would then miscount those leaving, and, of course, he wanted to earn something for himself as well.

Marek said that the money was not my problem, but I

kept looking for some way of getting out of it, because I didn't want to go, because I wanted to stay with everyone else.

Marek explained that I had "good" looks – I had blonde hair and blue eyes – that I had no accent when I spoke Polish, which meant that I could walk around town freely, and that I would be of more use to them there than here; but it still seemed to me that it would be simply desertion, and that they would die here, and I might survive there, and that I couldn't do it . . . Then Abrasza Blum joined in. He was staying with us at the time. He had arrived just after the second wave of deportations, I think on the evening of 19 January. He had sciatica and had to lie in bed, and have injections. He was in great pain.

He didn't speak much, he just smiled with that serene smile of his and said that it had to be done. And that it wouldn't be safe at all. But we had to have people over there who would take care of various things. Not just accommodation. After all, our weapons came from the other side, he said. So . . .?

And I said no more.

I had a lot of respect for him.

A few weeks before the second wave of deportations, somewhere around New Year of 1943, I wrote that piece, the last thing I wrote for forty-three years. Before the war, I had considered being a writer – it was to be my second career, alongside medicine. It was a sort of play, a dramatic monologue. About a grave digger who buried people in Treblinka, and who led his closest relatives to the gas chambers, I don't remember whether it was his parents, or his wife and children. And on New Year's Eve they all come back to him, those he saw dying, those children from Auschwitz, whose feet froze to the ground, and the pregnant women, the young and the old. All I remember from it is a line that repeated like a chorus, "wagons, wagons, wagons, rumbling trains on rails", and I don't recall any more. I only know that it ended with a voice calling out, or with a prophesy of revenge in the coming year, that it would end with the Germans living

above: Young orthodox Jewish boys, destined to be rabbis, studying the Torah in prewar Poland.
"Study children, don't be afraid
Every beginning is hard
Happy is he who learns the Torah
What more does a man need?"
From the Yiddish folksong "Oyfn Pripechok"
(Hulton Picture Company)
Right: The Star of David on top of the tram that ran through the ghetto indicated that it was in use for Jews only. *(Hulton Picture Company)*
Below right: Children on the streets of Warsaw in the early days of the German occupation, October 1939.
(Hulton Picture Company)
Below left: A bicycle rickshaw in the Warsaw ghetto.
(Hulton Picture Company)

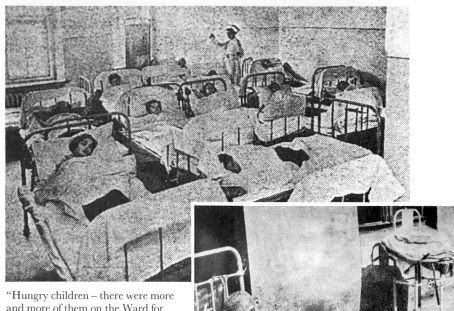

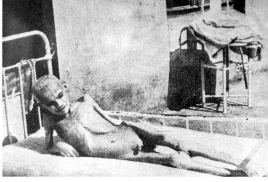

"Hungry children – there were more and more of them on the Ward for Internal Diseases, until, finally, they took all the beds." The Children's Hospital in the Warsaw ghetto. *(YIVO, New York)*

"'Oh, when my sister died, Papa said it didn't matter where they buried her because we wouldn't live to visit her grave anyway. Papa wrapped her up in paper and took her out into the street…'" The body of a dead child in a Warsaw gutter, taken from a passing tram, 1942. *(Adina Blady Szwajger)*

"When the children came back to the ghetto after begging, they'd slip in through a hole in the wall one after another." *(Camera Press)*

Caught in a round-up. *(Camera Press)*

The bodies of the dead are wheeled out of the ghetto on handcarts. *(Camera Press)*

Above: German soldiers walk through the blazing streets of the Warsaw ghetto in the aftermath of the Ghetto Uprising, May 1943. *(Camera Press)*
Right: Child with hands raised in surrender during the Ghetto Uprising, 25 April 1943. *(Associated Press)*
Below: The merry-go-round just outside the ghetto wall to which the author refers in her account of the Ghetto Uprising. *(Polska Agencja Interpress, Warsaw)*

The false Polish passport in the name of Irena Mereminska, back-dated to 1935, which the author obtained to replace the documents she lost in the Gestapo raid on the café in Miodowa street. The details read: Date of birth, 21 March 1917; Place of birth, Kielpiny; Occupation, student of biology; Height, medium; Complexion, fair; Hair, blond; Eyes, blue; Special Marks, none. *(Adina Blady Szwajger)*

The author's *Kennkarte* (identity card) in the name of Irena Mereminska issued by the General Government of Poland under German occupation on 27 July 1943 and due for renewal on 27 July 1948. This *Kennkarte* allowed the author to travel relatively freely in the course of her resistance work. *(Adina Blady Szwajger)*

Membership card of the Warsaw-Bialystock Medical Association, accrediting the author as a qualified doctor. This document enabled her to obtain the pass that allowed her and thirteen companions to escape from Warsaw after the collapse of the Uprising in October 1944.
(Adina Blady Szwajger)

Identity card certifying that Irena Mereminska is a soldier of the Home Army, 2nd Platoon, Medical Section, signed by the Chief Commandant of the Region, Radwan. *(Adina Blady Szwajger)*

The monument to the Heroes of the Warsaw ghetto which stands in open ground in what was the ghetto. *(Camera Press)*

through everything just the same as we had – with dying children and mothers and old people, and that they too would be wandering through empty streets . . .

Once when we read this together Abrasza said that it shouldn't be like that, that no one would take revenge on children and old people, and in any case that hatred of a whole nation was wrong. And suddenly I realized that he was right. I changed the ending to one in which there was "victory" and "never again" or something like that. He was someone who had a great influence on me. Therefore when he said that I should go I stopped arguing. I understood that in times of war orders are orders.

I went. With the work party.

It was the morning of 25 January 1943.

It was a beautiful sunny day. Frosty. But I felt hot. Beneath my brown overcoat, I wore three layers of underclothes and a nightshirt rolled up in such a way that it wasn't visible beneath my other clothes, a summer dress, a good-quality two-piece suit and a summer outfit. The outfit was very old, dating from my school graduation, but I didn't have anything better. In addition I had on two blouses and a cardigan. That I was able to do up the summer coat over this clothes store I probably owed to the previous three years. Although I had been spared the swelling which comes with starvation, I certainly wasn't overweight.

I carried a shopping bag with me and in it a spare pair of tennis shoes and certain other important treasures. There were photographs – lots of photographs – and a picture which I had painted for my mother when I was fifteen years old, and an ash tray of Danish porcelain, which had been saved by some miracle.

This most valuable treasure I lost only in the Warsaw Uprising, and to this day it is the only loss to which I cannot resign myself.

By chance, the only thing that survived was a picture from childhood. I still have it today. Painted on a yellowed piece of board, it shows the window of my room, with its crooked blind, and an amaryllis in a pot, and through the window, the view of the building across the courtyard, with the roofs of houses beyond that. A fragment of a dead world.

I went through the *Wache* without being searched, amid the crowd of Jews going out to work in factories on the Aryan side of the wall. I don't remember exactly which gate, but it was probably the one on the corner of Leszno street and Zelazna street. It must have been that one, because I remember that I found myself at once in the middle of a crowd milling around on the corner of the street. This was a crowd of spivs waiting to buy something cheap from the Jews leaving the ghetto, and extortionists on the lookout for potential blackmail victims. I heard them miaowing – that is how they used to let each other know that there was a Jew coming – but I immediately slipped off my armband,* and looked them straight in the eyes so calmly that no one thought to stop me. I just mingled with the crowd. Yes, it must have been on Zelazna street, because almost immediately I found myself on Zlota street. Maria Zarebianka, whose mother had been Mamma's nanny, and who was a friend of hers, lived there. It was to her that I went on that first day.

Hela Keilson, with whom I left the ghetto, stayed somewhere else, but I don't remember where.

But Maria – Maniusia as we called her before the war – welcomed me warmly, with tears, and well-concealed fear, because *Bekanntmachunge* – notices declaring that the penalty for hiding a Jew was death – had already been posted around the town. And they were not empty threats.

I sensed at once that she was afraid, so after greeting her, I immediately told her that I would only stay for one night. I said that I already had somewhere to go the next day, although I was not at all sure that it was true. I spent the night in her house on a mattress on the floor. She offered me

---

* "Outworkers", Jews who worked on the Aryan side of the wall, had to wear armbands bearing the Star of David while outside the ghetto.

her own bed, but I refused, because she was Mamma's age or even older.

She was not well off. She worked as a clerk for the tram company, and clerks earned next to nothing. For supper we ate whatever she had in the house. Bread and *Blutwurst* – black pudding. It was awful wartime stuff, but at the time it tasted delicious.

After I had gone to bed, she found an old fur collar in a chest, and sewed it onto my coat, because those who had escaped from the ghetto could easily be recognized by their lack of fur. The Jews did not have any fur because they had had to surrender it to serve the clothing needs of the German army. But not all of them gave their furs away; a few people sold them for a few groszy to the peddlars who immediately descended upon the ghetto when they learnt about the order to hand furs in, and others simply destroyed them. Mamma and I had cut up her fur coat and my fur collar, then burnt them piece by piece in the iron stove we used to warm our flat. Consequently, my coat had no fur on it, and the new fur collar meant a lot to me. Maria also told me several important facts, for example that newsboys would shout out warnings if there was a round-up ahead, but that you had to listen carefully, because they shouted out which street it was on while still running. She told me about the tram drivers, and about how you had to jump off if the tram slowed down between stops, because it meant that there were Germans at the next stop. We did not talk about the past at all, nor about my mother, nor about what had happened to me over the past few years. I left at six-thirty in the morning because Maria went to work at seven.

I never saw her again. Before the Warsaw Uprising I didn't visit her so as not to put her at risk, but I phoned her a few times at work. After the war I wrote to her from Lodz, and received a very cordial birthday card for Mamma's birthday on 1 December 1945, but I was unable then to go to Warsaw because I had a two-week-old daughter. I went to Warsaw in March 1946, but Maria had died a few weeks before, in

February. I felt guilty that I had not been able to thank her before.

When I left on the morning of 26 January 1943 I went to look round Warsaw. I had arranged to meet Hela Keilson at ten o'clock, so I had a lot of time to spare.

I went on foot. Somehow my legs carried me, from Zlota street to Marszalkowska street, along Krolewska street to the Saxon Gardens, then to Krakowskie Przedmiescie. I turned into Miodowa street as though I were going home to Swieto-jerska street.

But I didn't feel anything, although for all those days, months and years I had missed my own town, which was outside the ghetto walls. I didn't feel anything because I was still there, now and forever, behind the walls, in the middle of all that was going on, and this normal city was in some way no longer mine, or else I didn't belong here.

But during my first walk there was one moment when that walk could have been my last. Someone came up to me and asked me the time. That's all. I reached with my right arm to my left to expose my watch, and looked at my right sleeve – empty.

"I've forgotten my armband," I said instinctively, then froze in terror. But the man had not heard me, or perhaps pretended not to hear.

"Pardon," he said. I had already regained my self-control and as though nothing had happened I said: "Half past seven."

I walked on, my legs like jelly. I was afraid to look round. I turned into Dluga street and went towards Freta street, no longer in the direction of home, a home which, of course, I no longer had.

And then on Freta street I bought a roll. An ordinary, warm roll. I was hungry. I held it in my hand and didn't dare bite it. Perhaps I might draw attention to myself if I ate a roll in the street? I went into the entrance of a building and ate it – a real white roll. And then it occurred to me that I couldn't go on like this, that I had to shed everything, even my memories, and be, once again, a normal person on the streets of an ordinary city.

Except that the city had ceased to be ordinary.

It seemed too quiet, even hostile.

Some details have faded in my memory. I don't know when I met up with Marysia (Bronka Feinmesser), a secretary from our hospital. Was it the same day, together with Hela in the café on Miodowa street, or a day later? I don't remember our meeting at all, although we had not seen each other for a few months. It was as though we had never been apart, and had been everywhere together. But I do remember that when we met, we went together to the address that Marek had given me on Senatorska street near Miodowa street.

The man who for the next few months was to be my immediate superior lived there. He used to give me money and instructions.

We never got on well together. He was distant, standoffish, official, with a great sense of his own importance. Fortunately, after Marek joined us, and was staying with Antek (Icchak Cukierman), all of these matters were arranged with them. But that was much later. After the Ghetto Uprising.

It was still the first – no, already the second – day.

I met Hela in the café on Miodowa street near Krakowskie Przedmiescie. The café was at the front of the building. It was owned by Mrs P., the wife of an army colonel, whose surname I don't remember. She lived with her three beautiful daughters on the first floor of the same building. We spent the first few nights with them in a large communal room. We kept all of our belongings and money in a large trunk. After my aunt left the ghetto I kept all her money there as well, because she didn't trust the people she was living with.

After a few days we found somewhere to live. Hela and I managed to sub-let a room on Dzielna street near the ghetto, and we registered ourselves there officially, obviously on forged papers, which we had received straight away. But from whom? I don't know. Maybe from Peter, who used to supply identity papers, and who was already in touch with

Marysia? Or from our superior on Senatorska street? I don't know. And I don't even remember the surname on my false identity card, but I remember that on all my papers I had the same Christian name, Irena, and my mother's real name, Stefania, and my real date of birth. Everything else was false.

I remember that Hela was called Janina Pulawska, and that her father was called Leon Malecki in his false papers. I remember this clearly because I learnt of it later in an awkward moment. But that comes further on in my story.

From the first few days Marysia and I were almost always together, and we soon set about our work.

Our task was to find and prepare places to live for those who were to leave the ghetto, and to obtain papers for those who would be able to move about the town.

Our meeting place was the café on Miodowa street, and of the people who met there, I will never know who was the most careless. Many people besides us used to come to the café – those who forged papers, those who needed them, and many other people from the resistance, coming with all sorts of problems, some of them having nothing in common with us.

Hela was still very upset, and was too scared to go out. I know that she used to go to see her parents, for whom we had found somewhere to live on Wspolna street or perhaps Prosta street.

At first, I behaved very stupidly. I don't know whether it was courage, bravado, or thoughtlessness. At the very beginning I behaved as though I was still the same person as before, as though I still had some right to be on these streets and to mix with these people.

One day I went to the hairdressers on Dluga street where my mother and I used to have our hair done before the war. I went to the same hairdresser. I sat in the same chair, facing the same mirror, as though nothing had happened. Only the face that I saw in the mirror was somehow different.

The hairdresser behaved normally as well.

"Do you want to have your hair washed?" she asked.

Only later, while styling my hair, she leant down over me. "And your mother?" she asked me quietly.

I shook my head and said nothing.

"You have such manageable hair" she said, and we said nothing more to each other.

"You idiot, you trusting idiot," I said to myself after I had left. But that happened at the very beginning. Later on I would never have done it.

No, I don't remember much from those first days and weeks.

But by then nothing mattered other than my work.

It absorbed me totally.

In the morning I used to leave our room on Dzielna street to go and meet Marysia in the café. I don't remember where she lived at that time. We would eat our breakfast just like other customers in the café, and over tea and a bun we would make plans for the day. Frequently Peter, who, as I've mentioned, supplied false papers, would join our table, and often photographs would pass his way under the napkin, or birth certificates and identity cards would come in our direction. Sometimes he would give us underground news- papers.* From the moment that I hid the scraps of paper in my handbag or tucked them into my clothes the shivering began – a sort of fear or anxiety. It was a cold feeling beneath the skin – an awareness that from that moment on every accidental search in the street might be the end. And the day was just beginning.

We would go off to various parts of the city – Zoliborz, Powisle, Praga. So many addresses – where did we get all those addresses from? Someone once asked me, and I didn't know. Maybe from notices in the entrances to the blocks of flats advertising rooms to let? Or rather, more often, through the network of contacts with people who were "secure". Whenever we went to a new address, we never knew for

* Broadsheets and bulletins, probably produced by the Home Army.

certain whether it was genuine, or a trap, whether on leaving such a place we wouldn't meet the police, and whether the lives of the people we had lodged there would be safe. Every day there would be a meeting in a café in Praga or Nowo-grodzka street to pick up the next batch of photographs from our messengers, and sometimes to give them in return completed documents. Documents and accommodation – they were the most important things just then.

Just before the spring, when the Ghetto Uprising was approaching, and after Antek, Kazik, Bojowiec, Synicka, Ratapier and Michal Klepfisz had joined us, we started to transport guns and ammunition from one place to another, that is, from those who sold or provided them, to somewhere near the ghetto, from where someone else would collect them. I was least afraid when I carried a gun, because I knew that I wouldn't let them take me alive. Sometimes before leaving I would drink a glass of vodka on the stairs for Dutch courage and then go out. Tipsy. And in that tipsy state a patrol stopped me on Zelazna street and ordered me to open my bag. Hidden beneath the potatoes was some ammunition. Smiling broadly I opened the bag wide.

"*Los*," said the German gendarme. And I walked on.

But in fact that was when I really started being afraid, because several times I met people from the university, and a few of them looked at me very strangely. To avoid one girl, I jumped out of a moving tram. She was a member of the ND,* one of the most active in our year. I remember her well. Small, blonde, ugly, with a spotty face. But she had nice eyes, very blue. She was called Janka – I don't remember her surname. I got into the tram and only noticed her after a while. I was standing on the platform, and she was sitting inside the tramcar. Next to her stood a young man. I didn't recognize him, he wasn't from our college. She looked at me, and started to say something to him, looking all the time in

* Partia Narodowo-Demokratyczna (National Democratic Party): extreme right-wing and anti-Semitic political party.

my direction. I didn't hear what she said, but I didn't want to wait to see what happened next. I jumped out on the corner. I don't think anybody noticed.

Once I had been given some cyanide by my "boss" I was less afraid, because the worst thing I could imagine was that I wouldn't be able to bear the beating and that I would start talking. What I didn't know was that the cyanide was stale.

And as spring approached I came to realize that this was still my home town, and that many people still knew and remembered me, that all the time I was walking around on the same streets as I had done before.

At that time Dr Margolis worked as a nanny somewhere on Muranowska street, and we often used to go and visit her there. From the window on the stairs we could see the ghetto, and from there we used to try and spy out people we knew, but we never recognized anybody.

Usually I went everywhere with Marysia because it was safer. We used to walk together smiling and chatting like two young girls – just like all the other girls who filled the streets of Warsaw. But if one of us went out alone, she might forget herself, and have "sad eyes", eyes that betrayed the pain within.

I don't remember when particular people left the ghetto, but I know that by that time many people had already got out, including some of my closest friends and relatives. Some of them, like Dr Margolis, left soon after us, but when, for example, our friend Stasia, Welwl's wife, managed to get out I no longer know. I do know she did manage to leave, as did my aunt, and also some of Dr Heller's family – her nephew Bubi Aftergut, and her sister Judita Braude. Lodgings were found for all of them, but frequently they would be betrayed, and we would have to find them somewhere else to hide.

For Stefan, my husband, I found a place in a greengrocer's cellar in Mokotow. His parents, with his brother Mietek and his wife, had not wanted to leave the ghetto.

We had already learnt the awful lesson that when a prospective landlord wanted a lot of money it was very suspicious, as he might turn out to be an extortionist. But often there was no alternative, and we had to take a risk.

One day one of "our" people from the hospital did something disgraceful. It doesn't matter who. It might have been understandable if it had been to save a life, because people desperately wanted to live. But this was to save their money.

They sold us an empty flat – that is, we repaid them the deposit they had already put down on it – because they said that they had found somewhere more comfortable. Marysia installed Mrs Natanblutowa there, together with, I think, Judita Braude. When some people came to blackmail them, it became clear that this flat had already been betrayed. Fortunately all they took was money. I don't remember why, but a few days later, we had to spend the night in this flat – somehow it was unavoidable. There were several of us there, including Stasia. We sat together in the dark. Late that night someone, presumably the same extortionists, started to bang on the door. We sat quietly and in the dark, just as we had done in the ghetto. They banged a few times, but in the end they left. Everyone envied me because I had a terribly painful boil on my finger, and was oblivious to what was going on. I spent the night walking round, holding my hand up in the air. After we left the next morning, I went to Dr Skonieczny, who had been the Dean in our hospital, and now worked in the Omega Hospital on Jerozlimskie avenue, who lanced my boil. It was just like the Chinese proverb that says: "When you have toothache, get someone to hit you on the other side of your face . . ."

Individual events during this period between the end of January and April have faded from my memory. It was a sort of dream, a trance. As we were already on this side of the ghetto wall, our whole day was taken up running around trying to arrange various things. Sometimes it was money, sometimes weapons, or sometimes collecting people who were escaping from the ghetto. And somehow none of it seemed to matter. Because all of our feelings were concentrated on what was happening within the ghetto walls. I often went up to the walls with "deliveries" – we would throw things across, or receive things from the other side – and I remember how I dreamt at times that they might let me go back there.

On 17 April I was due to go back into the ghetto with Michal Klepfisz, because there was a lot to deliver. We were already in front of our entrance, when at the last moment I learnt that I was to stay behind. He asked me to remember about his wife Lodzia and little Irenka, and he went, while I had to turn back and go to Zoliborz. I burst into tears, but after a few moments I remembered that it was forbidden to cry on the streets.

A little earlier, about 9 April, Renia Frydman (Zosia) left the ghetto. She was the last from our hospital to get out. Just then we received that last letter from Dr Braude-Heller, the Head Doctor in the hospital, telling us that she had "other plans". By then it was already the night of 18–19 April. I slept with Hela Keilson in our room on Dzielna street, and in the morning we heard shooting.*

---

* The Ghetto Uprising, which was initiated by ZOB, lasted from 19 April until May 1943. Forces were uneven: 2,100 German soldiers, including SS troops, were confronted by 1,200 Jewish fighters armed with 13 heavy machine guns, some hand-held machine guns, etc. However, ZOB's main weapons were grenades and incendiary bottles (see Martin Gilbert, *The Holocaust*, London 1986). The longest resistance was offered by fighters in underground bunkers; the rest of the fighters were burned out of their hide-outs, some of them escaping through the sewers. According to Jurgen Stroop, the SS commander during the Uprising, 7,000 Jews were killed in the fighting and 30,000 were deported to the death camps. The whole area of the ghetto was reduced to ruins.

Chapter Ten

❖ ❖ ❖ ❖ ❖

CAMPO DEI FIORI

The shooting was coming from far away. It was not in our house, nor in our street. I put some clothes on and went downstairs, and I was told that it was in the ghetto. People kept saying: "It has started."

I went upstairs and told Hela about it, and she seemed to withdraw into herself. Her face was grey. I didn't even try to comfort her.

"I'm going out," I said.

"Go," was all she said.

I dressed myself very carefully. I put on my best two-piece suit, combed my hair, powdered my face and put on some lipstick. Just before I left I looked in the mirror. Everything was all right, just an ordinary face.

I bought a bunch of marsh marigolds from a flower seller. A big bunch. I held these flowers in both hands so that I could plunge my face into them. To remind me of joy and of spring. It was Holy Week. Monday.

I went towards Krasinski square to be as close as possible to my house. It was as though my legs carried me of their own accord to the wall of the ghetto.

There was a fountain there. It stands there to this day. Just an ordinary, bulky, squat street standpipe from the past.

At this fountain, in my childhood, I used to wash tears from my eyes and blood from my legs after I had fallen in the street or in the garden.

But today I didn't have any tears to wash. I just stood and leaned against this fountain which I knew from my childhood.

A merry-go-round had stood on the square nearby for

several days. A working merry-go-round. There were children sitting on this merry-go-round, while it went round and round, and I could hear the music playing. Maybe I imagined it? The children were laughing and the people going by were smiling. And on the other side of the walls you could hear shooting.

You could hear shooting, and the children were laughing. And I stood there with my bunch of marsh marigolds and smiled, just like everybody else. People said afterwards that there were flags flying, but I didn't see them. I didn't see them although truthfully I didn't shed a single tear. Even if I had been able to, and had wanted to, I wouldn't have cried because it was as if all the tears that I had ever had had dried up long ago, years before.

It wasn't something you could cry about. My legs were somehow wooden and heavy, and maybe I would have sat down somewhere if there had only been somewhere to sit. But there wasn't.

Milosz wrote a beautiful poem about this merry-go-round.* He wrote that it was just like at Campo dei Fiori where Giordano Bruno† was burnt at the stake while people were dancing in the square. Later, much later, when I read this poem, I thought to myself that maybe near this merry-go-round he had seen a smiling girl with marsh marigolds.

I remember nothing more of that day. I know that I had to leave because I had something to do – but sometimes it seems to me as if I have been standing there to this day.

Sometimes at night, just before waking up, I feel that my legs are heavy and I know that I am still standing by that pump on Krasinski square, and the merry-go-round is going round, and behind the wall my house is burning. Because that is where it stood. Right by the square.

---

* See p. 98.
† Giordano Bruno (1548–1600): Italian philosopher who was burnt at the stake for heresy.

And then I wake with a deep aching.

I didn't go to Krasinski square every day.

I used to go with Marysia to Muranowska street and look from the window on the staircase. We looked until our eyes hurt. But we couldn't see anything; in our eyes we had the greyness of smoke, in our mouths the bitter smell of burning which hung over Warsaw. Marysia and I were still the same smiling, carefree and cheerful young girls in the Holy Week of 1943. There was a lot of work to do because we believed that many people would survive, because not all of those who fought would die. We had to continue looking for rooms, preparing papers, while a blind terror hung over Warsaw, making it hard to find lodgings.

Soon afterwards it was Maundy Thursday. It was raining, so I put on my old suit and my tennis shoes, and went to the café on Miodowa street, and I left my best dress in Mrs P.'s flat. Marysia, Halina and Hela were waiting for me as we had arranged. But when I arrived, Marysia said that we had to go to Zoliborz straight away, because there was a room to let there that we had to see and organize.

Hela Keilson and Halina, Marysia's sister, stayed behind at the café, as we were to return very soon, and I think we arranged to meet them for lunch? I don't know. And we went. I don't remember whether we managed to arrange that flat, I only remember that on Invalidow square there was a round-up, so we had to wait, and we started to worry whether they would wait for us. In the end we caught a tram from Zoliborz to Miodowa street, but we found no one there.

The café was closed, the street was empty, and we walked by without looking at it to Senatorska street or Krakowskie Przedmiescie. Again we bought some flowers from the old women on Krakowskie Przedmiescie, and we walked back along Miodowa street with our flowers. There in front of the house next door stood the lady caretaker with a few other women, and they told us how the Gestapo lorries had come and taken everybody from the café, and had taken the owner and her daughters from the house, which they had then sealed up.

We walked on again, Marysia knowing that she would probably never see her sister again, and I that I might not see Hela. Apart from that, we were now left without any identity papers, because she was registered with her sister and I was registered with Hela, and we didn't have anywhere to live, because we couldn't go back to Dzielna street as Hela had that address on her identity card. We didn't have any of our things with us, just the clothes we had on, and no money to speak of – about three hundred zlotys in our pockets. Everything was left in the sealed house on Miodowa street.

We had to move Hela's elderly parents from their lodgings because Hela knew their address, and you couldn't be sure of anything, or anybody.

Once again we stood in Krasinski square and told each other jokes to make ourselves laugh. We were supposed to go to Senatorska street to tell them what we had arranged in Zoliborz. But we decided against it because we didn't know whether we were being tailed. We stood holding our flowers listening to the explosions, while Swietojerska street burnt and we stood laughing. I saw my own house burning. And I kept laughing.

In Krasinski square there was a tram terminus. We caught a tram to the railway station. We got on an electric train and we went to – I don't really remember where, probably to Swider?

We rented a room for one night in a guesthouse there, which, although it was almost empty, was being prepared by the owners to receive guests for Easter. We told them that we were looking for a place for our grandparents for the summer, because my grandfather had had pneumonia, and that we hadn't managed to get back to Warsaw before the curfew. They believed us – or maybe they just didn't want to ask too many questions, because they rented us a room without even asking to see our papers. The next day they agreed to give us the same room for a few more days and over Easter, as we had said that we wanted to find lodgings for our grandparents in Swider. In fact we did rent a room in Swider with a kitchen and a veranda for the old Keilsons, and we told everyone once again that they were our grandparents, and that the old man had just been ill.

After arranging these first few nights we had to go back to Warsaw because we had run out of money. We didn't have enough to pay for the next few days in the guesthouse, nor did we have any papers.

Back in Warsaw, as soon as we got some money from the people on Senatorska street, we set about trying to obtain some new papers. There was a local council clerk from Lodz, Jerzy Trediakowski, who when escaping from Lodz had taken some original seals and blank identity card forms with him. His wife had a laundry in Warsaw, so that he was easy to contact. He arranged our papers immediately, and in fact I still have that passport with a "Lodz" stamp in it, with my place of birth as Kielpiny, and my name as Irena Mereminska.* Mereminska was the surname of some friends of ours who had once lived on the other side of the river Bug, but were not there any more – some of them had died, and some of them had emigrated before the war, and anyway, anyone on the other side of the Bug was impossible to trace. For Marysia's papers we used the name of a friend of mine from college who had died before the war. We used these papers until the end of the war.

We got these new papers just after Easter, and on the same day we rented a flat for ourselves for the summer – a room with a kitchen and a veranda in Miedzylesie.† We used to go to Warsaw in the morning, and come back to Miedzylesie at night.

Miedzylesie was very convenient, because the curfew there was later, and we could make it home on time as long as we got to the railway station by eight o'clock, and anyway it was

---

* See illustration section between pp. 74–75.
† Miedzylesie: a small town to the northeast of Warsaw.

good to get out of Warsaw for the night. We kept these lodgings for the whole summer, right up to October I think, although by then we were already living at 24 Miodowa street.

We found this room on Miodowa street by chance just after we got our new papers, and we were registered there legally. Using the false passports Mr Trediakowski had given us, we obtained genuine identity documents and registration cards. The flat was self-contained, which was very convenient. But that is a long story, and everything that happened in Miodowa street happened later, in the period leading up to the Warsaw Uprising.

But for the moment the old Keilsons were safe, and we had somewhere to stay. The Ghetto Uprising was still going on. We had a lot of things to do, but every day we managed to go to Muranowska street for a while to have a look at what was going on. Once it seemed to us that we saw a red sweater on the roof of a burning house . . . The strangest thing was that for a long time, I think right up to 3 May, the telephone to the ghetto worked, and we used to talk to them in the evenings, but it was already clear that we had to organize an escape route for the survivors. Antek and Kazik were in touch with the sewermen, and we were constantly meeting people to discuss various things.

The sewermen worked for the City Cleansing and Sewerage Services and knew the layout of the sewers under the city. They were indispensable for getting people out, because going through the sewers without a guide was impossible. It was easier to fall into a storm water drain and to drown than to find an exit. But at the same time the sewermen were the worst extortionists. They were a real bunch of crooks. Their leader, whose office was somewhere on Kazimierz square, was simultaneously the leader of a gang of extortionists.

We had to force them to do it. To terrorize them. They were afraid of the resistance movement, so we told them that the resistance had ordered them to show the fighters the way out of the ghetto, and that the penalty for betrayal was death. They agreed.

It seems to me now as though that whole period when the ghetto burned, and everybody talked about it in the streets and on the trams, and said such different things, (some speaking with compassion, and others laughing that "They're frying the Jews"), and we always listened as though indifferent, always smiling, when we were always running somewhere with instructions to bring something or to organize something, or simply to arrange meetings between people – it seems to me now that it was all one terrible day. And it was devoid of any details. It was, I think, already 8 or 9 May. Then, when it was all over and Kazik had gone through the sewers to the ghetto to fetch the fighters, and everything was ready, I was told to go to Grzybowski square and meet Krzaczek, a man from the AL.* On my way there, I heard shooting from a distance. I reached Grzybowski square and there was Krzaczek. But he was already dead. I think that was the only time that I felt that I was going to faint, and I had to lean against a wall on the corner of Prozna street and Grzybowski square, because it seemed then that all our plans had fallen through, because Krzaczek was to have told me about the lorries that were supposed to come to the exit of the sewers on Prosta street.

But then I realized that I couldn't have known everything, that I was only a messenger girl, and I felt sure that those at the top, Antek and the others, wouldn't have left everything hanging by a single thread which could so easily be broken. And then I thought that I mustn't faint on the street, that it would be an idiotic thing to do, and I went on.

And in fact everything had been well prepared. On 10 May 1943 the lorries drew up at the exit of the sewers on Prosta street, loaded up, and drove off to the forest.

* AL – Armia Ludowa (the People's Army): the Polish Communist Party's resistance organization, supported by the Soviet Union and which operated separately from the much larger Home Army.

The ghetto was almost burnt out. The smoke and the bitter smell of burning hung over the streets of Warsaw. The next phase had started . . .

No, it is not quite true, it hadn't yet started. The next day, and the days after that, were still to come.

Abrasza Blum did not go to the forest. He was older than the others and not particularly healthy. He stayed in Warsaw.

He "belonged" to Wladka, one of our girls, and I think that she probably arranged a room for him on Barokowa street. Or perhaps we found it for him. I don't know.

The next day Wladka told me that Abrasza wanted to see me. I wanted to see him too, but I would never have suggested it myself, because it was against our rules to go somewhere when it wasn't absolutely necessary. But I went because he had asked me.

He was full of joy. Not just cheerful, but joyful. Like a man who has come out of a dark nightmare into the sunlight.

We talked a little. Just chatted about nothing in particular. And in the end he told me why he had wanted to see me. It was as though he was embarrassed by this childish desire, and he was ashamed to tell Wladka.

He dreamt of cakes. Real cakes from a patisserie. I left there very relieved. For the first time for several months I smiled. Really smiled. It was as though the sun had also started to shine a little for me. Those closest to me had survived, and I thought that they were safe in the forest. And that conversation, it was so "normal".

The next day I thought all morning about our meeting. We had arranged to meet at two in the afternoon, but by twelve o'clock I was going around the patisseries and looking for cakes which in appearance and taste might remind him of real prewar Warsaw cakes. I bought some. And with a little box done up with coloured string I found myself on Barokowa street punctually at two o'clock.

But it had already happened.

Earlier that morning the caretaker had locked the doors of the room and had gone for the Gestapo. Abrasza jumped out of the window. From the third floor. He didn't die instantly. He broke his legs. And that is how they took him.

What prevented me from going up the stairs and falling into the trap I don't know. I don't remember. I remember only that with this superfluous box dangling from my finger I returned home and I had only one thought. I mustn't, I mustn't cry. So once again I smiled at people with a grimace which apparently looked like a real smile . . . And it was still going on – still happening – my own private Campo dei Fiori. And there was something else. Hatred. Such an awful hatred of murderers and informers, greater than my despair.

I came home to Miodowa street without the cakes. I had lost them somewhere along the way. But even when I got back to my own room and closed the door behind me, I wasn't able to cry.

*　　*　　*

I don't know all the details – I don't remember everything, nor did I know everything at the time – so I can't and I don't want to accuse people by name. But I know that apart from the partisans from the AL there were other groups fighting the Germans in the forest, such as the NSZ, the National Armed Force which was derived from the ONR,* the Radical Nationalist Camp. They were part of the extreme right wing of the National Democratic Party, who before the war had been fascinated by fascism, and had shown an instinct for anti-Semitism. So when Jewish fighters were killed in the forests in skirmishes with people other than the Germans it was easy to conclude who else had been involved. For security – relative security, that is – a "safe conduct" was necessary, a certificate from the High Command stating that ZOB was a part of the Home Army (AK)†.

* ONR – Oboz Narodowo Radykalny (Radical Nationalist Camp): nationalistic right-wing political party.
† AK – Armia Krajowa (Home Army): owed its allegiance to the Polish government in exile its plenipotentiary (Delegatura) in Warsaw.

I was only involved closely in these matters because at that time I took Antek's place in carrying messages to Henryk Wolinski. This was at his request. He had a Jewish wife, the beautiful Pani Kruk (Mrs Raven), so called because of her jet black hair, and they lived in their prewar flat in the Aleje Niepodleglosci. She never left the house, and at that time she was going through a depression and was even scared of visitors. She wasn't afraid of me, however, as we had met previously through Tosia Goliborska, and she felt safer because I was a woman.

I had to go to Henryk's house several times to obtain the safe conduct from the High Command of the Home Army which was supposed to ensure a degree of safety to those in the forest.

Henryk was very upset by his own powerlessness in this matter. I felt so perplexed by it that at times I tried to cheer him up.

But in the end we had to take some of our people out of the forest. Some were transferred to another area, and some were brought back to Warsaw.

Somewhere along the way Celina met up with Antek. Wlodek (Welwl Rozowski) and Marek moved into a flat together.

* * *

It is like a recurring nightmare.

I am walking along a street in Warsaw – I know it is that street. Sniezna street? Yes, I think so. I see the entrance to the building I am to go into, when round the corner comes a motorcycle with German soldiers on it. I know. I know with absolute certainty that they are going to the same address. And that now everything depends upon me. Will I get there before them? I run, but my legs are paralysed, and I am unable to move. I run, but I stand still on the same spot. And they are getting closer all the time. I grow cold . . .

It's just another one of those dreams after which my heart aches.

Even after all these years we have never gone back over the events of that day. I have never asked Marek what he felt during those hours or days when he sat alone in a betrayed flat and waited – for either the extortionists or the Gestapo. And before that he was waiting for Welwl, who had gone out to get some money.

Some extortionists had come to the flat in which Marek and Welwl were both hiding. They demanded money. A lot of money. More than they had.

I don't know how they persuaded the extortionists to take what money they had and to come back later for the rest – after all, we never discussed it again. Welwl, who looked a little "better" than Marek, left the house to fetch this money. He never came back.

Yes, someone was to blame for that death. Someone who had taken fright, someone who was afraid to keep a young man with "bad looks" in his perfectly safe flat for the few hours that were supposedly necessary to organize the money. Someone who ordered him to go out into the street and come back in a few hours time. At dusk. But at dusk Welwl did not come back.

They caught him somewhere on the way, and they shot him.

But it wasn't just the owner of the flat who took fright – I did too. Marysia came the next morning from Senatorska street, looking very pale. "Wlodek was killed," she said. "But Marek stayed behind." (Wlodek was Welwl's codename, and even between ourselves we used these new Christian names.) I got up and took my bag as though to leave. "You can't go there," said Marysia, who was always so sensible and practical, "you might fall into the trap. And he may no longer be there anyway."

I became cold with fear. I sat down. I listened to her common sense.

"I am going to Janina's," Marysia said as she left, "I'll

send her there." I sat curled up on the sofa, with a sweater on. I was still cold.

Marysia came back. She said: "Janina has already gone," and so we waited, and I was still cold. Marysia couldn't stand it any longer, and shouted at me: "Stop shaking, damn you!"

Janina returned after about an hour, perhaps two? I don't know, after all it seemed longer than life itself.

She said that "so far" everything was all right. I stopped shaking. I stood up and went out. Only then. Marek was waiting there for me. In the meantime Marysia ran off to arrange the place I was to take him to. I don't remember now where we went.

I remember that we walked along clinging together like lovers. And I think that we didn't talk, because what was there to talk about? I asked him if he had a gun with him, and I was no longer afraid. Because fear is always a part of defencelessness.

After Wlodek's unnecessary death, hatred was once again stronger than grief. We had to keep smiling, and looking into each other's eyes.

That was the end of the Ghetto Uprising, and the beginning of everyday existence. The everyday existence of a courier girl for ZOB.

On Miodowa street.

CAMPO DEI FIORI

In Rome on the Campo dei Fiori
baskets of olives and lemons,
cobbles spattered with wine
and the wreckage of flowers.
Vendors cover the trestles
with rose-pink fish;
armfuls of dark grapes
heaped on peach-down.

On this same square
they burned Giordano Bruno.
Henchmen kindled the pyre
close-pressed by the mob.
Before the flames had died
the taverns were full again,
baskets of olives and lemons
again on the vendors' shoulders.

I thought of the Campo dei Fiori
in Warsaw by the sky-carousel
one clear spring evening
to the strains of a carnival tune.
The bright melody drowned
the salvos from the ghetto wall,
and couples were flying
high in the cloudless sky.

At times wind from the burning
would drift dark kites along
and riders on the carousel
caught petals in midair.
That same hot wind
blew open the skirts of the girls
and the crowds were laughing
on that beautiful Warsaw Sunday.

Someone will read as moral
that the people of Rome or Warsaw
haggle, laugh, make love
as they pass by martyrs' pyres.
Someone else will read
of the passing of things human,
of the oblivion
born before the flames have died.

But that day I thought only
of the loneliness of the dying,
of how, when Giordano
climbed to his burning
he could not find
in any human tongue
words for mankind,
mankind who live on.

Already they were back at their wine
or peddled their white starfish,
baskets of olives and lemons
they had shouldered to the fair,
and he already distanced
as if centuries had passed
while they paused just a moment
for his flying in the fire.

Those dying here, the lonely
forgotten by the world,
our tongue becomes for them
the language of an ancient planet.
Until, when all is legend
and many years have passed,
on a new Campo dei Fiori
rage will kindle at a poet's word.

CZESLAW MILOSZ

Note: This poem, written in Warsaw in April 1943, was first published
in the underground anthology *Z Otchlani* (From the Abyss, 1944),
dedicated to the Jewish tragedy by poets living "on the Aryan side."
The anthology reached New York in spring 1945. Because there were
several reprints and handwritten copies which changed the text slightly,
there are various versions of the ending of the poem. These differing
versions also appear in the translations into Hebrew. In this edition
the probable first version is restored.

Chapter Eleven

❖ ❖ ❖ ❖ ❖

24 MIODOWA STREET

We rented the room at 24 Miodowa street in the spring of 1943.

It was a big, light room, painted a lemon yellow colour. In the corner, near the window, there was a big bed made of boards, covered with paper mattresses. On the bed lay two pillows and an eiderdown bought in the flea market, covered with bed linen, which was in turn covered with a paper bedspread, the sort that you could buy during the war. On the wall above the bed was a similar paper "tapestry" and on that hung a picture of Our Lady of Czestochowa. Just below it, also on the "tapestry", the small picture that I had saved from our house. It had been in the room on Dzielna street, where I had spent the first few days with Hela, so I hadn't lost it with all my other things above the café at the other end of Miodowa street.

Beneath the bed we kept a second set of mattresses for any guests who had to stay the night.

In the opposite corner, also near a window, stood a bureau or desk, a very useful old piece of furniture from Pociejow.* At the foot of the bed stood a small wardrobe – we did not have many clothes or much linen, and didn't need anything larger.

In the middle of the room stood a round table. Or rather the top of a round table, put on top of a square one. Between

---

* Pociejow: an estate in Warsaw belonging to the family Pociej surrounded by the market. A synonym for cheap and tatty goods, hence "furniture from Pociejow".

these two table tops there was a hiding place in which we kept all our papers. Our money was kept in another hiding place, cunningly stuck on the underside of the shelf in the wardrobe. There were four ordinary chairs at the table, and in the corner behind the curtain a bowl and two buckets (the water tap was in the corridor), and a small electric oven with two rings. Above the oven there was a shelf for pots and pans, while the frying pan stood on the stool – all of these things had come from Pociejow.

This building is still standing today; it now houses the Theatre School. Our room is still there, but the entrance to the building is now from 22 Miodowa street. I went there once a few years ago. Perhaps for old times' sake? Probably. It was a marvellous place. Before the war this building had housed the Supreme Administrative Court, but afterwards the judges' rooms in the courtyard had been converted into self-contained flats with a communal toilet and a water tap in the hall.

But there were even greater advantages in living there. At the front of the building there were several offices which belonged to the gas and electricity companies, and to some other businesses, which were constantly full of hundreds of customers. It was an ideal place for a contact point, and as soon as we realized that we might be able to rent this room, we immediately sought permission, and found the money to pay for it.

By what miracle this safe house survived until the Warsaw Uprising I don't know. But survive it did.

I lived there with Marysia for the whole of 1943 and half of 1944, and we were both registered there. The place was known to many people as an ultimate refuge in case of danger. And people did come there. Briefings took place there every day, people used to come to collect money and newspapers, to bring papers, or sometimes without any reason, just to talk and chat for a while – an hour or so, just to feel like human beings again in this huge city, in which there was no room for us. Frequently somebody whose flat had been betrayed would come to spend the night with us. We would pull out the mattress for our guest from underneath the bed on which we both slept. The room was on the first floor, and under the window there was a wooden rubbish bin, so that in case of danger we could jump out of the window in relative safety.

As our frequent visitors, especially the men, might have attracted the attention of our neighbours, we used to throw loud parties in the flat. They were jolly and alcoholic. We had a record player and a few records, and we used to make a lot of noise going out into the hall to fetch water for tea. In short, girls having fun.

Sometimes "high level" meetings were held there. On those occasions one of us would stay to act as hostess, the "guests" would bring flowers, while a lookout would sit in a café on the other side of the street. And then Christmas Eve and New Year's Eve! Everybody who was able to move around the town – and even some of those who would normally stay at home – would come. A moment of relief. A meeting of those lonely people, for whom the illnesses caused by being locked up led to depression. And meetings between friends. Moments of light during this everlasting nightmare.

This is how I see that room on Miodowa street in my memories. But forty-five years have passed since then, so perhaps everything was different? Yes, many years have passed, many things have faded from my memory, and I don't really remember the sequence of events. That is why everything I write is so chaotic . . . It all happened – but when? I don't really remember. Only that it all took place in the period before the Warsaw Uprising. So it must have been for a year – or maybe a little more than a year. Because afterwards there was the Warsaw Uprising – the hospital in the basement of the house on Miodowa street, the escape through the sewers to the Srodmiescie, the city centre, and finally our escape from Warsaw.

But that is another story . . . and I will return to it later.

For the time being we were at 24 Miodowa street.

The whole of my past is like a film tightly rolled up and

hidden in a drawer in the dimness of my memory. Only if you happen to touch this roll, the whole film unwinds and shows individual frames. Some of the images are faded, some are wiped out. But they are still there. Sometimes it seems to me that it is all still happening, that we are still living in that time. That is why I have not been able to live as others do. Like those who went out into the wide world and started everything from the very beginning. They know how to enjoy a car, a flat, the comforts of everyday life. Or even to enjoy life itself. It doesn't matter, certainly not now. What is important to my story is what happened then. What a normal day was like.

The everyday life of a courier girl.

A foggy day in autumn. October? November? Certainly the autumn of 1943. We were no longer living in Miedzylesie.

I wake up. It is unpleasant. I have an awful feeling that something unpleasant is going to happen. Marysia has already got up. She has put the water on for tea. In our household Marysia is sensible, domesticated and caring. I don't cope well with the small necessities of life.

"Get up! You have to leave soon," Marysia says to me.

I know now. It is the beginning of the month, and I have to collect the money from Senatorska street. One million zlotys. Not just a huge sum, but also an enormous package of paper money. One thousand 1000 zloty notes, or two thousand 500 zloty notes. I dress appropriately, putting on two layers of clothes. One pair of knickers with an elastic around my thighs underneath my suspender belt, the other pair on top. And two blouses, the one underneath tightly drawn into the waist with a wide belt.

And also a shopping bag with a false bottom. Lots of girls in Warsaw had such bags. These were the bags used by the resistance, messenger girls' bags. The people in the street knew about them, but the Germans never seemed to realize. They were dangerous if you were caught in a round-up, but in my case, if I had been caught with such a large amount of money, it wouldn't have made any difference.

And dressed like that I went to Senatorska street. The money was already there, and my "boss" tried to hurry me. He wanted me to get out of his place with this burden as soon as possible. I was in a hurry. I suddenly realized that I was putting all these packs into my underclothes and down the front of my blouse into my knickers while he was standing and looking at me, and that neither of us was the least bit concerned by it. Neither he nor I. As if he were not a man, and I – as if I had never been a woman.

I left. It was muddy. On the way I went into a baker's to buy something to put in the bag.

Walking up the steps to the small shop on Miodowa street, I slipped in the mud and fell to my knees. For a few moments I knelt in the mud, frozen with terror. I was afraid that one of the packs of money might have slipped out. I got up as though I were made of glass. But everything was all right. I reached home. At home the most convenient place to lay out the money was on our bed. So I took off my clothes, or rather put a nightdress over my underclothes, rolled up the eiderdown at the foot of the bed and put the packs of notes around myself. If somebody came unexpectedly, I could draw up the eiderdown quickly around myself and pretend that I was just lying in bed on that sad autumn morning because I had a cold.

So I sat among this vast sum of money, counting it and dividing it up into piles.

For Wladka . . .

For Celka . . .

For Krysia . . .

For . . .

And the biggest pile – for Marysia and me.

Every pile was the only means of support for fifty to a hundred people for a month. Whereas for me these piles of somebody else's money were just pieces of paper. Dangerous pieces of paper at that. It was probably then that I started hating money, or perhaps not hating it, but ceasing to value it. Once and for all. We had to get rid of these pieces of paper as soon as possible, because they might cost us our lives.

Even now I am unable to keep or to value money. But now it doesn't matter.

I divided up this money and put it into piles, wrapping up each pile separately, and then covering everything with my eiderdown, and the paper bedspread.

Marysia and I waited for "our people". This time she stayed to keep a lookout, while I went out to do some shopping. On days when we gave out money, or when we had things to discuss, we prepared lunch for everybody. People had to eat something, and preferably not in a restaurant. That day it was my turn to cook.

I bought a loin of horse and some potatoes. Roast horse loin was one of the few dishes I was able to cook as I had never really learnt to cook. I don't have a talent for it, but it mattered to me. I really did my best. For that reason the day that Celek joked at lunch that I cooked like a doctor, that is exactly according to the prescription, and that what I cooked tasted as though it were from a prescription, I was offended. I think that was the only time that I came near to quarrelling with him.

"Find yourself a better cook, or go to a restaurant," I snapped at him. And no wonder – I was tense, everything seemed to me evil and hostile. It was simply through fear – fear enough to last not just for that afternoon, but for the next few days. Until all the money had reached its eventual destination.

Lunch finished, we went out separately. At intervals of several minutes. I was last.

First I went to Praga street. On Argowa street lived a family, just two people, mother and daughter. They were staying with a working-class family, pretending to be relatives expelled from Germany. The mother worked somewhere as a servant, I think. The daughter was fourteen or fifteen years old. Her father had been found lodgings somewhere else.

The girl was pale and sad. She milled around anxiously, as though she wanted to tell me something.

"What's the matter, Mirka?" She blushed, perhaps from a lack of confidence? "Well, tell me, I'm in a hurry."

"I would like something to read," she stammered finally. "There is nothing here!"

I didn't know what to say. I wasn't allowed to go too often to the secret addresses, as it could be unsafe for those who were hiding there. But I couldn't refuse her. She was an intelligent girl. For her, books were as necessary to life as bread.

"I'll bring some, for sure."

I managed to keep my word. On several occasions I brought her a few books I had bought in a second-hand bookshop.

For some reason we had to separate her from her mother. They had to change their lodgings, because the neighbours had started to be suspicious, and I lost direct contact with her. Marysia used to visit her, but I don't remember whether she mentioned anything about books for Mirka.

In one flat after another I saw the same thing: pale faces, sad eyes, hands stretched out for those few zlotys, a signature on a small card, and on my way. Then more meetings on the street. Around dusk, a banknote handed over secretively in the entrance to a building. A receipt taken from a shaking hand. Quickly, quickly. Soon it would be curfew. I had managed to give out today's portion, and went off home on the tram.

Not until I reached home did I notice that I had given someone too much money. Two banknotes had stuck together. I don't know who I had given it to. Well, of course, I would have to give it back out of my own money. It happened occasionally; fortunately, quite rarely. Marysia was not yet home. I was anxious about her. But I set the table. Two plates, bread, something to go with the bread, two glasses, and a bottle of vodka.

Marysia came in just before curfew. Pale.

"What happened?"

"I was nearly caught in a round-up. With the money."

There was no comment. Just vodka. Just the two of us. And if it was just the two of us, then just a few glasses of vodka. But if one of the boys came for the night, we would go on until we were dead drunk.

But that day it was just the two of us, and in the morning we had to be sober. Because in the morning we had to start distributing the money again.

It was the same every month. The first two, three, sometimes four days of the month were always like that.

Just before the Warsaw Uprising, when people already knew that something was about to happen, we used to distribute tinned food and candles as well. I didn't manage to give all of it out. I was left with 50,000 zlotys, a few tins and a few candles. The candles and tins were useful in the hospital during the Uprising, but the money I left in the Old Town.

What was so memorable about that particular day? I don't know. Maybe it was the fall in the street, or perhaps that silly argument with Celek?

That particular day wasn't the hardest, or even one of the hardest. It was normal. Just like any other day. Apart from giving out money, we had lots of other things to do. We had to visit people and arrange things for them, to go and see our own families so that they did not feel isolated, or to help those who found themselves in difficult situations. We had constant problems with lodgings and papers. Every so often somebody would be betrayed, or "burned" as we called it, and we had to move them to new lodgings. There was not much time left to us for thinking or for remembering what happened.

Very little time was left for our own "private matters". These went on despite everything. After all, we were still young. Marysia had met the love of her life. Zygmunt was a well-known Warsaw lawyer, who now worked as a locksmith, and lived with some awful old woman on Krakowskie Przedmiescie. Once he came to us very upset, and told us that his landlady was afraid to go up to the loft with the washing, and had asked him for help.

"Because it might be haunted by that Jewess. At the beginning we hid her in the loft, but later, when they announced that they were giving the death penalty for it, we gave her up."

My "personal affair" – Stefan – was hidden in a greengrocer's cellar in Mokotow street. There was a tap in the cellar, and the owner kept her stock of vegetables there. She used to go there every day as though to collect her goods, but at the same time she brought him something to eat, and took out his bucket. While she was in the cellar he could walk about in his stockinged feet, but the rest of the time he had to lie in bed. I used to go with her every other day, as though to buy something, and we used to speak quietly to each other, while she spoke loudly to me. At first, he was full of hope, but afterwards he said he couldn't bear it any longer, so when he had the chance to escape via the "Hotel Poland", he decided that he would go.

"One way or another . . ." he said. I couldn't convince him to stay or talk him out of it. And that is how my first love came to an end, and my first marriage. But that was later . . .

In the meantime a perpetual cycle of the same problems went on: running around from seven o'clock until curfew, always on the streets, rushing from one meeting to another. Sometimes we would meet in cafés, where we would sit for a long time drinking coffee and eating cakes, and would hand over photographs for identity cards, receive papers, or newspapers, and then once again we would have to distribute them to all of our addresses. There were hundreds of stairways and floors, and we were not allowed to ask directions. I learnt them all so thoroughly that when someone gave me an address, and the number of a flat, I already knew which courtyard and which staircase it was on. It was a sort of sixth sense, and I was virtually never wrong. There were incidents which were almost miraculous. One day I went into a stairway, where someone was registered on the third floor, and on the first landing I saw Mrs A. S., a lawyer from Cracow, with two extortionists. They were checking her papers, and didn't want to let her go. I think that she didn't have enough money with her. I went past her twice, so that she would notice me. I wondered whether she would have the presence of mind to keep them talking for a while.

The building was next to Mr Strojwas' office. Before the war he had been one of my father-in-law's contractors. I think he belonged to the ND, but during the war he behaved decently, as least as far as we were concerned. He used to employ some thugs, I don't know what for. I think he was involved in some business with the Germans – I don't know. I ran off to his place, and he sent two of his men, who got there in time to chase the others off.

Unfortunately, that wasn't the end of it, because they knew her address, and she had to move to new lodgings. However, her life had been saved.

Sometimes we would win through by impudence and ignorance, as happened to me on one occasion. I was coming back on the tram from Stasia's place in Grochow. When I got off the tram at Castle square, and turned into Miodowa street, a *Volksdeutscher* stopped me – "*Jude?*" At first I pretended that I didn't understand, and then I went the whole hog, and led him to the police station on Dluga street. I went up to the policeman and complained that this man had accosted me in the street, and I asked that they check his documents. So they checked his documents and mine – of course, I had a real identity card.

"What do you want from this lady? All her papers are in order," the policeman said to him. Later I discovered that this man had followed me from the flat in Grochow. He was a friend of the landlord's son. They had pointed me out to him because he had wanted to earn some money – just to earn some money. And he was so confounded by my impudence that he thought that he had confused me with somebody else. But if I had known who he was, I would probably have paid him, and would have arranged for the flat to be changed. As it was, nothing happened.

One day, Jozef (Natek), one of our fighters, was caught. He was one of "our people". And we will never find out whether he told them, or whether they already knew, about everything. They took him with them to all the many addresses and they took people away from all of them. A lot of people died as a result. He knew our address on Miodowa street. We should have changed our lodgings, but we couldn't because we didn't have anywhere to go. There was nowhere we could go without putting others at risk.

So we stayed at home. We spent the whole night waiting to see if they were going to come for us, and drinking vodka. But nothing happened. Jozef jumped out of a third-floor window as they were leading him to another secret lodging. And so we knew that he hadn't betrayed our place.

And that is what everyday life was like: people, problems, forever running around – and fear. Already then there was fear. Every familiar face was hostile. The whole town, my town, my own town, that I had grown up in, was strange, hostile, and every corner I turned might be my last. But this fear was subconscious. It was underneath, hiding. It was only because of this fear that we drank so much vodka. In the evenings. Even near the very end, when Marysia moved to Leszno street, I used to drink on my own. Because it wasn't possible to go through with it any other way.

Chapter Twelve

❖ ❖ ❖ ❖ ❖

MIEDZYLESIE

In the summer we used to go to Miedzylesie. In 1943 we went from April till October, but in 1944 we came back to Warsaw in a hurry on 29 July. To be there on time. Because already we knew that something was going to happen. The Uprising. We wanted to be with everybody in Warsaw. And we were there, until the very end, until 11 October.

But that is another story.

We used to go to Miedzylesie for the night, and come back to Warsaw at seven o'clock in the morning. It was the room we had rented when the café on Miodowa street was "burned" in April 1943, a room with a kitchen and a large veranda, large enough to sleep on. It had a separate entrance, not through the landlord's flat. This made it convenient for us and for our frequent guests. People used to come to us there as well. Above all our families. But also Zosia and Joanna, two of our girls with whom I spent the last two months before the Warsaw Uprising. Celek was a frequent guest there and on Miodowa street, as he seemed to be "burned" frequently, and had to keep changing his lodgings. There were also incidental guests who came from necessity.

This address should have been kept secret – but it wasn't.

As a rcsult we had an experience that could have come from a silly adventure film.

One morning we left the house to catch the train, at the last moment as usual. Out of the bushes in front of the house emerged an entire family. Five people – two children, their parents and their grandmother. They had been hiding in some sort of shelter in Warsaw, where they were threatened by extortionists. They managed to buy their way out, but had to leave their lodgings.

I don't know where they got our address from, but they arrived on the first train. Scared of coming into the house, they waited in the bushes until we emerged.

We were in a hurry to get to Warsaw.

We let them into the house, locked the house up and ordered them to stay silent until our return in the afternoon. We promised to come back at two o'clock. And we went off to Warsaw. I don't remember why we had to stay in Warsaw only until lunchtime on that particular day, rather than until the evening. I know that we hurried back, and that by midday we were at the railway station in Warsaw. Earlier in the day there had been a terrible storm, and when we got to the station we learnt that the electricity lines had been damaged, and that for the moment the electric trains weren't running. They were supposed to repair the lines soon, and we were told that the trains should be running in about an hour.

We waited for an hour before it became clear that it would be much longer. And those people locked up in the house! What were we to do? We decided to go on foot. It was nine miles from the tram terminus. Not a great distance, but when we had gone about a mile a thunderstorm started. I don't think that I have lived through a storm like that before or since. It was completely dark, only the lightning flashes every now and then lit our way. The lightning struck around us again and again. We were going along the railway tracks, next to which ran the high-voltage lines. Every so often lightning struck the pylons. The rain came down in torrents, and we could see nothing. But worst of all was the wind, which blew in our faces and made walking difficult. The lightning flashes cast our shadows in front of us on the track, and it looked strange, as if we were in a film. But we really were afraid, not like in the cinema. When we reached Wawer, we met some linesmen in a hut, who advised us not to go any further because it was dangerous. But we had to get home, so we walked on. Our dresses stuck to our bodies like bathing costumes. They were made of the sort of material that shrank, and so they really looked like swimming costumes. We were constantly wiping our faces with our hands, but it didn't help, whatever we did the rain would pour over our eyes and blind us. Lightning struck nearby, and all the lights in the houses near the railway line went out. It had struck the power station at Falenica. It became completely dark, as though it were night. We managed to go on by feeling our way along the railway lines.

Finally we reached the station at Miedzylesie, and there we found ourselves in a funny situation. On the station there was a small sweetshop, whose owner we knew well. In her hut there was a candle burning. We knocked at the door. We wanted to dry out a bit and to have something to drink. The lady opened the door, looked at us and shouted: "Jesus and Mary!" We didn't understand what had happened and we carried on our way. Later we discovered that the colour in our dresses had run, so that when we wiped our faces we were smearing them in all the colours of the rainbow. It must have looked very ghoulish, and by candlelight it gave the impression of blood.

We finally reached home at about eight o'clock in the evening, terrified at the thought of what we might find. It turned out that our landlords had realized what had happened, had opened the doors and had taken care of our "guests". They had given them some food, and helped put the children to bed. They didn't utter a word of reproach. They really were exceptionally decent people. Unfortunately, when I went back to Miedzylesie after the liberation, hoping to thank them, I couldn't find them. I never did find out what happened to them.

One day, on my way back from Warsaw to Miedzylesie, I noticed something suspicious. It was a Saturday, and we were coming back earlier than usual, in the early afternoon. At the station in Warsaw we noticed a young man looking at us. We thought we had seen him before at the station in Miedzylesie.

He got into the same wagon as us, but into a different compartment. We decided not to get out. At Miedzylesie we just looked out of the window. He got out and looked round. He looked in the direction of the windows of our wagon, but we moved away from them in time. The train moved on. We decided to go to Swider to visit the Keilsons. At Swider we looked round carefully and set off initially in a completely different direction. But we couldn't detect anyone tailing us. It may be that we had imagined the whole thing.

We used to go and see the old couple fairly frequently, because we felt sorry for them. Dola Keilson had died in Otwock, and Hela was in the Pawiak prison.* It seemed terrible to us that two old people should be left so alone in life. They lived in a detached house and had a nice room with a veranda. When we came in through the garden gate Mrs Keilson was sitting on the veranda, knitting.

She turned round and shouted loudly: "Alexander!" It was enough to scare us, but not as much as when we heard the old man's bass voice resounding over the whole house.

"How many times have I told you, not Alexander but Leon!"

It was no surprise when we had to find them other lodgings. Fortunately we succeeded – at Jozefow. We repeated the story that they were our grandparents. It was easier to find summer lodgings there than in Warsaw.

We lived in Miedzylesie until the end of July 1944, in the last few months with Zosia and Joanna. (At this time Marysia was already living in Leszno street.) They moved into my flat on Miodowa street, because for some reason their lodgings had turned out to be unsafe.

I was betrayed only once, and that was during those months, together with Zosia and Joanna. The extortionists must have been well informed, because no amount of impudence on our part helped, and they took us straight to the

---

* Pawiak prison, named after Pawia street, was the Gestapo prison where political prisoners, both Poles and Jews, were held.

police station. It cost us ten thousand zlotys. We always carried that sort of sum with us in case we were given away. It meant that I was "burned", and I couldn't go to Leszno street again, because there, hidden in a flat by Marysia Sawicka, was the entire staff of ZOB.

I should write something, if only a few words, about that flat in Leszno street, and about Marysia Sawicka, who to this day is one of our closest friends – no, that doesn't express it – Marysia, who before the war ran in the 800 metres at the Skra stadium,* is a mother, a sister and a friend. She is old, older than me, she is ill, but she still travels the world to visit those few people who are left. Not long ago she was in Israel. She knows everything about everybody, and recently she told me that we are keeping her alive with the knowledge that we still need her. Her sister, Anna Wechalska, who was like her, and who gave her dead daughter's papers to Wladka, is no longer alive. Marysia lives modestly and quietly in Lodz. But at that time she was the main tenant in that three-roomed flat, which she shared with Antek, Celina, Marek, Stasia, Bernard, I think Kazik, and several others. She used to do all the shopping, going out with fear in her heart as to what she might find on her return. It felt like a real home. When you went there you forgot that you were in hiding, it was so peaceful and happy. Marysia would never say that she was scared, and I think that she wasn't afraid, although she could have been killed with us at any moment.

She is just the same today, always smiling. When we talk, we reminisce about various events, but she never says that she was afraid.

After I had been betrayed, together with Zosia and Joanna, I stopped going there. For the most part, Marysia took over my affairs. But that was much later, just before the Warsaw

* Skra stadium: a sports club and athletics stadium in Warsaw, still in use today.

Uprising. For the moment we had many things still before us.

I'll try to recount some of them.

❖ ❖ ❖ ❖ ❖

Chapter Thirteen

VOYAGES

When we had to go to Cracow we would go to the station not knowing which train we would catch. It was all down to chance, because in Radom the gendarmes might order everybody out, whereas in Radomsk the partisans might blow the train up. And so we would travel by whichever train we were able to catch, and we had to count on luck.

We were thought to be smugglers, because people going to Cracow used to take moonshine (home-distilled vodka), as it was more expensive there, and sausages. This was smuggling. We didn't take moonshine, but we always had one or two kilos of sausages with us. On the way the moonshiners used to pull out their flasks, we used to join in with our sausages, and so we travelled as a group of smugglers. I used to go with Kazik – Symcha Rajtazer. He looked like a real Warsaw rogue, the sort that comes from Powisle or Wola. But he was very young, not yet eighteen, and didn't know how to drink. Once he got very drunk on moonshine, and when we got off the train he sat on the stairs of the railway station in Cracow, and was unable to go any further. It would have been funny, especially as he became rather merry, and started to sing. Except that I was not in the mood to laugh. I was terrified. There was nothing else I could do. I left him sitting on the step, and went with my heart in my mouth to where the horse-drawn carriages stood.

"Please sir, could you help me?" I asked the oldest cabby. "My brother has got drunk, and I haven't the strength to lift him. And besides, I can't go home with him in this state, our father will murder him when he sees him drunk. We'll go for a ride, and he might sober up."

My voice was full of genuine despair.

"Get in, Miss," said the cabby in his soft Cracovian lilt. Together we hauled Kazik up on to the seat, and drove off. We had hardly started when Kazik leant his head on my shoulder and dropped off – phew, I heaved a sigh of relief. We drove around for an hour. Somewhere along the way, on Harowiska street I think, which we had gone down several times already, Kazik suddenly awoke with a start.

"What? Where? Where are we going!" I squeezed his hand. The never-failing routine of the underground worked. He shut up.

"How do you feel?"

"Fine," he pretended.

"Then we're off home. Golebia street, please, cabby."

We got out on the corner "so that our parents won't see us". Of course, we went off in a completely different direction. To Florianska street, I think, although I'm not sure. I don't remember the exact address of our contact point, but I do remember the entrance through an arcade to a photographic studio, and the display of photos of soldiers from the *Wehrmacht*. Among them one large portrait of a very handsome Gestapo man with a death's head emblem on his cap.

And a shop sign in German.

This studio belonged to a *Reichsdeutscher*. He had a Jewish wife, and there in Cracow she was protected, as in the capital of the German province of Poland the law still had some value. Their two children were also on the *Volksliste*, and the scene was beyond belief – the old Jewess sitting in her room behind the studio, with her son in the uniform of a *Hitlerjugend*.* It couldn't be imagined in Warsaw!

Things were very different in Cracow. I think they were a lot easier. If you were caught in a round-up there it was enough to wave some documents under the noses of the

* *Hitlerjugend*: Nazi youth organization.

gendarmes and to walk on boldly – and they would let you go.

But, despite that, people in Cracow seemed to be more afraid than those in Warsaw. Whenever they saw a patrol three streets away they used to turn around and go in a different direction.

But there were also many brave people in Cracow who helped us. Usually we went to Maria Hohberg (Marianska). Once I gave her some of my poetry and later forgot about it. After the war I found one of my poems in a book under the title "The Song Will Survive" as being anonymous.

Cracow was not the only place we used to visit. We also used to go to the camps in Trawniki and Poniatow. We almost lost one of our girls near Trawniki. She was caught near the camp, but managed to lie her way out of it, saying that she only wanted to buy and sell things. The guards were Ukrainians who liked their vodka, and let her go in return for some.

And I remember that when she came back, after being away for three days I felt her arms and legs to make sure that she was really alive, and that she was still in one piece.

I also used to go somewhere near Czestochowa, where there was a group of fighters living in a farmer's barn. I went there a few times to take them money. I saw Czestochowa as it was during the war, full of pilgrims, kneeling on the street or rather walking on their knees to the monastery. And I remember the monastery in the distance, on the hill, and the streets full of people, kneeling and praying. It made a great impression on me, because at that time everything supernatural had somehow become closer. Perhaps more necessary?

At the farm I used to go down the ladder to their hiding place beneath the barn, where we used to have scrambled eggs and vodka. Afterwards I would dress all of their small wounds, burns and scratches, because that was my "speciality". I would leave them a stock of bandages and cream, and return to Warsaw.

I was lucky that one of my trips didn't take place. I

was to go to Lvov with a Polish girl who was supposedly trustworthy. I didn't know her, and she wasn't one of my contacts. We each had two thousand US dollars* and a hundred thousand zlotys. I collected this money from Panska, where the ZOB Command was living at that time.

The two thousand dollars was just a piece of paper so it was easy to hide, but the hundred thousand zlotys was in 500 zloty banknotes, and I was completely papered with them beneath my clothes. I set out like this early one morning, as soon as the curfew had ended, but despite that met three patrols on my way.

When I got home these banknotes were soaked in sweat. From fear. I remember that I was most worried about the two thousand dollars, because if I were caught, I would lose the "real" money because of the stupid hundred thousand zlotys.

I didn't go to Lvov because I didn't get a pass. We hadn't managed to arrange it. It turned out that the girl had betrayed us. She did it for money. If I had gone with her I wouldn't be writing this now. That's for sure.

Even after the Warsaw Uprising we used to go to Cracow. I remember that once the Germans threw me out of the carriage at Zyrardow, and I travelled the twenty miles to Grodzisko on an open wagon in the freezing cold. There were still open wagons in those days.

I was lucky that someone had come to meet me at the station in Grodzisko, because I was unable to stand or even get up without help. Fortunately, I didn't get frostbite.

---

* These US dollars would have been in Poland since before the war or were smuggled into the country during the war, to aid the underground and Jews in hiding.

Chapter Fourteen

❖ ❖ ❖ ❖ ❖

IN THE RGO HALL

My meeting with this other world, with the children of the street, was strange. I don't remember how it was arranged, but in the winter of 1943–44, I found a job as a childminder in the Hall* of the RGO,† which was in the monastery of the Salesian Fathers in Powisle. The Hall was in the administrative wing. In the office of the monastery there was a telephone which I was allowed to use, which was very helpful at times. Besides that I had a real *Ausweis*,‡ which would also be useful. Although in reality I worked there only in order to disguise my real activities, I carried out my duties conscientiously, and I admit they gave me pleasure. This contact with children from the streets of Warsaw brought a little joy into my life; there were even moments when I forgot about my strangeness, and about the fact that I was constantly acting.

I played a small part in the difficult life of these poor creatures, so damaged by the war, maybe in a different way, but just as severely. They were not well fed or good tempered, they had no real homes or loving parents, and for that reason I felt close to them. They were very grown up, with that cruel premature adulthood of those whose childhood has been stolen from them.

Yet they were still children. One day we prepared a sing-

---

* Swietlica: a hall in which school children are looked after between the end of school and going home (i.e. a play-centre).

† RGO – Rada Glowna Opiekuncza (the Main Council for Charity): a legal charitable institution.

‡ *Ausweis*: identity card.

song, which was to take place in the evening – before the curfew, of course.

The boys asked me to come that evening (my hours of work were usually between ten in the morning and one in the afternoon). I told them honestly that I was afraid. Going home just before the curfew through the dark streets of Powisle wasn't safe. What I normally carried with me was too valuable for me to risk its being stolen. You have to remember that on the streets there roamed, apart from the gendarmes and the extortionists, bands of young men completely corrupted by the war, preying on anybody, not just us. The words "Get out of your coat, Miss" were not uncommon, and you were rarely able to resist. In this way Dr Margolis was deprived of her coat on the Mokotow Fields one frosty evening. Fortunately they left her with her muff and her papers. They didn't used to take papers. After all, the bandits were Polish, and didn't want to expose their victims to any additional danger from the German side. My fear was well founded, and increased by the darkness on the streets.

Unexpectedly I was offered a solution – a promise that I would be looked after.

"Don't be afraid, my dad's the biggest thief on the whole of Powisle – we'll take you home, and nobody will touch you."

They were not empty words or boasts.

A few days or weeks later I became convinced that we – the workers from the School Hall – were under the particular protection of the crafty fellows from Bednarska street, Furmanska street and Gesta street.* One day my own affairs took me to Furmanska. Somewhere in the third courtyard of some terrible slum there was a flat that I had to get to. But somewhere by the entrance to the first courtyard I heard steps closing behind me.

* All three are districts renowned for their criminals – pickpockets, burglars and petty thieves.

For a moment I felt cold with fear. But there was no way out. I couldn't go back, nor could I go to my goal, because I didn't know whether I was being followed by some common thief, or by an extortionist.

I went straight on, thinking that I would try and confuse my pursuer by going to a different staircase.

But somewhere between the second courtyard and the gate I heard a male voice with that characteristic Warsaw twang.

"Leave off, Felek, you motherf . . . You peabrain, can't you see she's from the Hall."

A sound of steps hurriedly fading in the distance, then peace. But I didn't go that day where I was supposed to go to. Better not to let people follow me there.

My work in the Hall did not last long, only a few months. Everybody who worked there was young, and involved in some sort of underground activity. One morning when I came to work I found the Hall empty. The previous afternoon they had taken the priests and all the staff from the Hall.

I am sure that those who lived in Warsaw at the time still remember those bodies hanging in black priest's habits, on the empty ground of the ghetto, visible from beyond its walls in Leszno street. That is where, in the spring of 1944, the Nazis hanged the Salesian Fathers.

Chapter Fifteen

❖ ❖ ❖ ❖ ❖

MR ANTONI

Mr Antoni was a caretaker on Prozna street, at number 12 or 14, I don't remember exactly. I know that both these houses are still standing today. They are identical, and their entrances look just the same, as do the caretakers' lodges, small rooms in the entrance, in which, before the war, the caretakers used to live.

Mr Antoni was, as he said of himself, "a Sergeant-Major in the Polish Army", and at that time it meant in the Home Army. He used to wear a sheepskin coat, always undone like a cart driver's, and had a long bushy moustache. Between his moustache and his bushy eyebrows he had the red nose of a drinker and a sharp pair of eyes.

In Mr Antoni's room there was a hide-out. In a small hole behind some packing cases people who had been "burned" could be hidden for a few days, and that was where we used to hide the young men coming back from the forest until we found them somewhere better to live.*

The courier who was our contact with the people in the forest was Zygmunt "the Needle", so called because of his job before the war when he had been apprenticed to a tailor. It was he who introduced me to Mr Antoni.

I used to go to Mr Antoni's quite often. Our relations were somewhat complicated. Mr Antoni used to suspect that I didn't want to mix with him, and thought that was why I used to refuse to drink his home-brewed vodka from a dirty

---

* After the Ghetto Uprising surviving Jewish fighters were moved to the forest, then, later, moved back to Warsaw again.

mustard pot. Indeed, I wasn't attracted by the prospect of that sort of drinking bout and I used to excuse myself, saying that I was on duty, that I hadn't finished my work, and that I had to stay sober. But one day I was unlucky. It was the day of the raid on the bank's van. I should have realized that he had taken part in it, but it didn't occur to me. When I walked into his room there were several people there. On the table stood mustard pots, and home-brewed vodka and beer. Sausages lay on a newspaper. Next to the food and drink lay the money. A lot of money. Mr Antoni was drunk. He grabbed me by the hand.

"If you don't drink with me today," he said, "it means that you despise the caretaker. And that's the end between us."

I knew there was no way out. I sat down. They poured a mixture, half vodka, half beer, into a mustard pot. I drank it . . . The world started going round before my eyes. I wasn't a delicate girl, but I have never drunk such a mixture before or since. Tears welled up into my eyes. I was unable to utter a word. Mr Antoni, delighted, clapped me on the back.

"We haven't got anything else here," he declared. "Let's go to a bar."

It was impossible to refuse. He was drunk and not in control of his faculties. In broad daylight we walked together across Grzybowski square. A fairly elegantly dressed girl with a caretaker in a sheepskin coat, his hat at a rakish angle, walking in a not entirely straight line. We went to a bar on Grzybowski square, where the theatre stands today.

We went in and sat down by a table. And a miracle happened. Antoni said that he had forgotten his money.

"Sit here and don't move."

He left me while he went to fetch the money. The barman wasn't stupid. He knew Mr Antoni. He winked at me and let me out the back way on to Twarda street.

"I'll sort it out with him," he said.

I don't really know how I managed to get home. That was my last meeting with Mr Antoni.

A few days later, when Zygmunt and some of our boys went to see him, a terrible thing happened. There were a few people from the Home Army there as well. Did someone inform? Did someone see? The German gendarmes came and the shooting started. No one got out alive – there were casualties on the other side as well.

Mr Antoni died with a weapon in his hand together with our lads. I don't know who the Germans came for. For our lads? Or for the others? In any case, they all fought together and died together.

Chapter Sixteen

❖ ❖ ❖ ❖ ❖

SUCH A SHORT HOLIDAY

Tadeusz was a really good-looking young man – tall, well built, with auburn hair, and dark blue eyes beneath long girlish eyelashes, and a charming smile on his tanned face. I was sitting in the café over a black coffee, when he came up to my table and asked in a low melodious voice: "You don't by any chance have yesterday's newspaper, Madam?"

I forgot for a moment that the arranged answer was supposed to be "I haven't looked at the date, but it must be an even earlier one." I murmured something under my breath. Not until Tadeusz stopped in his tracks, not knowing whether to sit down or not, did I come to myself and answer correctly. After a while we talked as though we were old friends, and for a moment the thought struck me – it's a pity that I can't allow myself a little flirtation.

Tadeusz was warm, but at the same time serious. He was supposed to be a new messenger with the Polish underground, and was to help us arrange papers and find lodgings, particularly for the young men coming in from the forest.

It was always more difficult to find lodgings for men, let alone fighting men, than for women, especially for women with a "good" appearance who spoke perfect Polish. So my attitude towards the new "helper" was enthusiastic, especially as he had so much personal charm. After a short conversation I passed Tadeusz a few photographs and addresses hidden under a newspaper. These were to be used to make new identity cards. In return he gave me the latest underground bulletins.

"The next meeting will be in three days' time in Simon's Passage, near the cinema."

"See you soon."

A smile and a languishing glance.

I stayed at the table. In a few minutes I had another meeting. This time with two of "our" girls. They came into the café laughing and smiling, as they were supposed to.

"May I . . ."

"Yes, certainly."

Then a mutual offering and lighting of cigarettes.

This time they passed me some photographs. And in return they got, folded in a paper napkin, a small sheet with the address of a room where they could lodge someone.

"Thank you very much, nice to meet you," they said politely. I went out into the street. I stood for a few moments in front of the nearest shop window – fortunately a milliner's – to check that I didn't have a tail.

All clear. On I went, in quite a good mood. After all, a meeting with a handsome young man, even for a loving wife, is still an event.

Those three days passed very quickly. A brief meeting in the street, at which we both arrived with the obligatory punctuality, left an equally good impression.

He gave me several sets of forged papers, made quickly and faultlessly, as I confirmed when I got home.

"When will the next time be?"

"Not for ten days. I am leaving for . . ." at the last moment I realized that I couldn't tell anybody ". . . Radom, on a private matter."

The story about my aunt in Radom, who every now and then provided her niece with some tasty tit-bits, poured out freely.

I did in fact leave the next day – for Cracow.

After my return I felt like someone who had been hit on the head with a truncheon. It had turned out that Tadeusz was an "agent provocateur" working for the Germans. The people living at the addresses he had found out about through me had been betrayed. From our contacts with the Polish underground we learned that those providing him with papers, and several other people, had also been caught. I was one of his very few contacts who had escaped.

He had been sentenced to death.

For the moment I was "burned", or even worse. I was myself under threat of capture, and posed a threat to everyone I met.

Fortunately Tadeusz didn't know my name or address, and didn't know the truth about me. As far as he was concerned I was a Pole helping those Jews still in hiding.

I had to go into hiding myself, to change the district I lived in, and to avoid showing my face in the streets. It was difficult, very difficult.

My "good" appearance and my local accent did not help. I was legally registered in Warsaw, so I couldn't register anywhere else.

And how to explain my continuous sitting at home? It was necessary to find a hiding place where I could at least partly explain my situation to the landlord.

Our solution was crazy, against all the principles of the underground, but it worked.

Joanna and Zosia worked as mothers' helps in a house in Mokotow. Their employers knew only that they were two girls from good homes who had been expelled from Germany. They were treated as members of the family, they ate with the family, and had to listen to the constant complaints about Jews who had no scruples about putting at risk the lives of decent people. It was a "patriotic" and extremely right-wing family, a combination making for the greatest philistinism one can imagine.

I used to go to visit the girls there, and I never aroused the slightest suspicion.

The family earned their living making fudge wafers and the lady of the house needed girls to help her make the fudge, and then distribute it to sweetshops and patisseries.

They were told as much about me as was necessary to

awake in them the desire to fulfil their patriotic duty, by helping a messenger from the Home Army who was in danger.

I moved in with Joanna and Zosia – they had their own room in the basement – and for three weeks I had the most improbable holiday! No duties – no meetings and no news about betrayals and difficulties. Hardly ever going out of the house (going only to the local shop, and that in the evenings), I occupied myself by helping the girls in their cleaning, I learnt to fry hamburgers and make meatballs for the numerous members of the family, and apart from that I helped with making the fudge – a horrible sticky mixture of sugar, milk and, I think, vanilla. We had to boil the muck while mixing it for hours, then pass it through a sieve, and then spread it on to wafers and put it under a press. All I got out of it in the long term was a dislike for fudge, and a healthy respect for the hard work of pastrycooks, especially on the day that Marysia, who used to come and visit me from time to time, stepped with both feet on to my whole day's produce! In a frenzy, I had to go and buy fresh ingredients, and start again. Yet in a way it was a real holiday. But it was also a painful meeting with the hypocrisy and prejudice of the supposed intelligentsia – not the lower orders this time.

Without regret I heard that the sentence on the charming louse had been carried out. I returned home the very same day – just like any other day, in which time was measured by the number of meetings, the number of things arranged or not dealt with. There was no time left for thinking, and certainly none for reminiscing or being sentimental about the past.

It may seem odd, but when I returned to this "normal" life, inseparable from its sense of danger, its continuous fear, in the streets and at home, fear which sat in your stomach like a lump of ice, I felt better, quite well even.

We had a sense of unity, through our awareness that we had to do this, that things had to be this way, and that it all had some sense.

We did not feel sad. We were still able to laugh and joke

about things. Perhaps because we didn't really believe there would be a future? I don't know . . . But I know that those days, when I used to go to Panska and stay for the night, or when the young men came to visit us on Miodowa street, remain in my memory as moments of light. We used to help each other – with vodka. But it was difficult.

At this time I was becoming increasingly anxious about Stefan, who was losing hope and strength of will.

And those who lost hope . . .

There were many such people. And the worst thing was that it was always easier to help those one didn't know. To lie to them. I always knew what to say to those in hiding, or in shelters.

But not to him. Perhaps if I had been able to it would have ended differently? I will never know . . .

Chapter Seventeen

❖ ❖ ❖ ❖ ❖

HOTEL POLAND

We walked through the streets of Warsaw on 11 July 1943 as we used to in the past. I walked on my husband's arm across Marszalkowska street, through the Saxon Gardens to Niecala street, down Wierzbowa street and Bielanska street to Dluga street. It was like 1937–39 again, when he used to take me home after the cinema, before that mad wedding on 27 July 1939. Except that now I was taking him from his cellar at the greengrocer's in Mokotow to the Hotel Poland. It was a small hotel on Dluga street, by the cinema.

We walked together for the last time in our lives. Although it had been his decision, it was I who led him along that last road. He had decided that he had had enough. That it was impossible to go on. One free place had been offered to us by Jewish Gestapo* men, who were trying to restore their credibility at the time, and I don't remember how it was allocated to me. In any case, I didn't think that I would be able to use it. There was no one else, so I told Stefan about it, and he latched on to the idea. It was as though it were his last hope, or possibly he was fully aware of what would happen. But he did not want to go on, he didn't even want to live.

I don't remember what we talked about, or even whether we spoke at all on the way. When we got there, someone at the porter's lodge checked his papers, or maybe gave him new papers, or took some from him?

* Jewish Gestapo: the Gestapo unit established in November 1940, officially known as the Office to Combat Usury and Profiteering. It consisted of Jewish policemen.

I don't know, I don't remember. I do remember that it was a small dirty hotel on Dluga street, but it seemed enormous to me at the time.

They gave him a room somewhere upstairs. That I know for certain. They didn't even check my papers. The place was full of people who had come to see off their relatives. When we got out of the porter's lodge and into the hall, it was as though we were in a dream or in a surrealist film. Everywhere there were Jews, without armbands, moving around freely.

These were rich Jews, because the voyage was expensive. Papers sent to people whose cremated bones had long since fertilized the ground of Treblinka were being resold by the Gestapo for large sums. It was an expensive death. Except that beforehand this money bought you two, three, or four days of illusion. Maybe that was in itself worth something?

The people I saw there were not starved. Hope had led the women to dress in their best clothes and paint their lips, and most of them had managed to go to the hairdresser's and have their hair done. I don't remember whether they were allowed out of the hotel, or whether there was a hairdresser on the premises.

There was definitely a café, where it was possible to drink coffee. It tasted like dishwater, but the café was always full. People got drunk on this foretaste of freedom and suddenly remembered that they were people. They talked – normally, loudly. They were free to go up and down the stairs as they pleased. They could spend time looking after their children and even tell them off, because the children ran around and made a lot of noise, as though they had been let out of a cage. And I saw children who were actually smiling.

I started to see everything more clearly, I saw not just this handful of children who had been "saved", but all of those who were already dead, those closest to me. But I didn't understand, even to the end. I had a feeling of foreboding.

Marysia was there as well, as one of her friends was also going. For those few days we went there daily. On the last day we didn't go home. We stayed the night.

And again I remember almost nothing. I know that we sat through that night of 12–13 July on a sort of settee somewhere upstairs on the landing.

"I won't say goodbye to you lest it be a bad omen for our next meeting after the war" is all I can remember of what Stefan said.

In the morning he just waved goodbye to me and went downstairs.

"Don't see me off," he said.

"Take care," he shouted from downstairs.

And he went out into the courtyard.

I ran after him. Marysia too.

And we saw. We saw that it wasn't buses taking them away but prison lorries. The gendarmes were collecting people up and shouting: "*Schnell, schnell!*"

And the people still didn't understand and were hurrying and pushing forward to get into the lorries.

We were nearly collected up with the others.

But we got out. Straight into the hands of an extortionist. He took us to the police station on Hipoteczna street, but our faces seemed so composed that the policeman didn't even check our papers. Because we were composed, composed as one can only be in the face of a disaster.

Because we already knew.

And I knew, I knew beyond doubt, that it was all over. And that I had done it to him, with my own hands. Although he had wanted it, if not for me he wouldn't even have known that this could be his escape from life.

The convoy went straight to Auschwitz.

Someone threw a note from the window of a lorry.

And once again we had no time for thinking and no time for that luxury which once was called despair.

We had to return to everyday concerns.

And my everyday concerns were the affairs of man.

Chapter Eighteen

❖ ❖ ❖ ❖ ❖

CHILDREN IN HIDING

It may sound silly, but somewhere underneath I still felt myself to be a doctor. Being a doctor sets you apart from normal life. It means that you always have to think of other people's pain as though it is something more important than your own. You are a doctor in order to help people and not in order to be sentimental about yourself. In any case, when there is so much pain around you, enough to fill the world, it is different from being alone with your private disasters.

Around me there was so much pain that if it had been divided among everyone in the world, there would have been some left over.

And then there were the children.

Writing about the children is the hardest part, because these are just words. I am not a woman of letters – and I cannot make the words cry out.

In any case this is not a piece of literature. This is an account of what really took place. When you say simply that a child died, it really doesn't mean anything. So many children died of hunger, so many were gassed . . . so many, so many . . .

Six million people died, and the sun didn't cease to shine!

And so why am I writing about this one baby? Because for between four and six months the young woman would hardly ever get up from her straw bed in the cellar, and she used to put my hand on her stomach and say: "It's alive! It's moving, isn't it?"

There was nobody waiting for her. She didn't have anybody

136

in the world. But she had this child in her belly, and that was her whole world.

She gave birth without any noise. Not a single groan. But she bled where she had bitten through her hands, and her nails were broken.

She gave birth to a live child. A girl. In the autumn of 1943.

Children are always being born. Even in hiding places and in cellars. But they often die, and it is not always possible to save them. You have only your own hands, but you also need medicines, and mother's milk, which in this case did not flow at all. The landlady was afraid to bring home more milk than she usually bought. And you also need air, of which there wasn't any in the cellar, and which you can't bring in your hands.

And they mustn't cry. The landlords were afraid. Those living with her were afraid. The harassed, terrified mother covered the child's face with a pillow. Because someone had come into the house. So it was no wonder that I had to carry the body of the newborn baby from the house in a cardboard box.

A different mother's child, an older baby, a few months old, I carried out in my arms in its swaddling clothes. But I don't wish to remember how I had to drink vodka with the undertakers before they would bury the body somewhere under the wall. And then I promised myself that if I were ever able to do something about it, children would not be born in hiding places.

There were live children too. Few of them were with their parents. They were already grown up, with that maturity of five- or six-year-olds which taught them that you must never cry, that you must never talk, and that almost all day you have to lie in bed, on a pallet.

Lying on a bed all day in some dark hole, children soon stopped walking. It is a recognized illness, called *rachitis tarda*,* or late rickets. But you have to see it to know what it

* *Rachitis tarda* (late rickets): a condition caused by prolonged immobility.

is like when a twelve-year-old girl lies without moving, and even when she is allowed to get up, she is unable to stand on her legs. And she cries without voice. And what it is like when the contractures start, and to watch all this helplessly.

It was only after the war that those who survived received Sterogyl, and a few returned to health.

But there was something else as well. The small four- and five-year-olds forgot how to talk. Their development went into reverse. They were like tiny animals looking with their enormous eyes, and letting out intermittent cries. They did not even know how to play.

When we returned to Warsaw in January 1945 I worked for the Central Committee of Polish Jews on Targowa street. One day I went with a team of Russian health inspectors to get the children out of their hiding places, because I knew the addresses.

When they were carrying out little Benio, the officer, who spoke a little Polish, because he came from a Polish family called Krynski, asked me: "This is a mentally retarded child, isn't it? An imbecile?" And I think that I didn't answer him at all, I just shook my head to indicate that he was just another child from the shelters.

There were other children as well, those without parents. Small beggars in rags sneaking under the walls of the houses in the evenings and knocking at doors to ask for a piece of bread. Reactions varied. Sometimes they would be given something to eat or even some rags to wear, but often, very often, they were chased away from the doors like animals – perhaps from fear? Probably. But sometimes it was different. Sometimes they knocked at the right door. They were brought in and would be passed along a chain of people of good will, until they ended up in our hands, or somewhere in the country, or in a monastery. Those found by us would be hidden in the safest places, those not found by anybody would perish.

And then there were the little newspaper boys. This is a very charming story. Because the Jewish newspaper boys were hidden by their little friends, the newspaper boys from the Aryan side. Even I never knew exactly what their hiding place looked like. It was somewhere in the ruins on Miodowa street. Their protectors would not allow me anywhere near the hiding place itself. They said that although they trusted me this was by far the best way. I used to come at the appointed hour to the ruins and just stand there. It was always at dusk. Suddenly they would swarm around me. Small figures coming out of the shadows, like rats. They hardly spoke. They used to come up to me and allow me to touch them. The oldest used to take the money and the few sweets I had been able to buy. And then they would disappear again without a sound. Just like rats. I never knew how or where to.

They survived up to the Warsaw Uprising. Beyond that I don't know.

There were two boys who spent the summer in a dug-out in the garden of a ruined house in Mokotow. We were told about them late in the autumn or at the beginning of the winter. They used to go to some people in Mokotow who would give them food, and we went there to look for them. It was nearly Christmas, and there was a Christmas tree in the house which reached all the way up to the ceiling.

The children weren't there. We asked the family to tell them, when they came, that we would come back for them in two days' time in the evening. We came back as we had arranged. We waited for them on a dark and narrow street. Suddenly the darkness was lit up by a beam of light from a torch. Terrified, we moved into the shadows – and we heard the voices of children.

"It's us, please don't be afraid."

We saw two small figures, black against the white snow, two ragamuffins with a torch.

We ordered them to put it out immediately and to walk on. We walked behind them looking at their tiny silhouettes, easily visible on the snow, as they walked onwards into the unknown. They stood and waited for further instructions on every corner. We had our hearts in our mouths. But we made it to their new lodgings, which were, I think, on the third floor of a house on Chmielna street. We got there without any problems. The good, kind Mrs Jadwiga, whose surname unfortunately I don't remember, started by giving them a hot bath and by burning everything that they had on.

We had to pay for the lodgings, but their guardian turned out to be a good honest person. The boys survived the war and later left the country. First they wrote a diary. They wrote about how they had survived for almost a whole year in a dug-out in Mokotow, fed by the inhabitants of the surrounding houses. They were cold and hungry and a little afraid, but the most important thing in their story was something completely different. A scooter. A scooter which they had found in a rubbish dump and had returned to working order with the help of wires and string. They used to ride it along the streets of Mokotow, forgetting all about being careful until someone reported them – "There are Jews riding on the streets and disturbing the peace." And so the gendarmes came. And the boys fled on their scooter. When they thought that their end had come, they found an old lady in their way with a stall selling apples. As they ran past her she knocked over her stall under the feet of the gendarmes. The apples scattered and the old lady started to despair and lament.

A furious gendarme threatened her with his whip but somehow she managed to get away. And the boys managed to get to their hiding place. And for some reason the Germans didn't want to wander around the dark streets of Mokotow. For three days the children sat in their dug-out without any food or drink. Only on the fourth day did they regain enough courage to go out and beg. A few days later we picked them up. Their diary finishes with the words: "And those ladies brought us to a nice place and we like it here, but we miss our scooter, because now we will never find it again."

Jasia was five years old when her mother – a doctor – died

of typhus in the ghetto. A Polish lady took the child to Czestochowa. But a few months later she brought it back to Warsaw to its aunt, saying that people in her neighbourhood had started to be suspicious. The child couldn't stay in the house where the aunt worked as a nurse. Dr Wierzbowska came to our aid. A dozen or more children owe their life to her, because she managed to arrange for them to be hidden in the house of a certain Father Boduen. Jasia went on a summer camp while we were looking for somewhere for her to stay. We found the very place for her with Mrs Janina, about whom I have already written, the same one who had done so much for us. But when Jasia came back from her summer camp, as she was about to go to her new guardian, it turned out that she had come back from the camp with scarlet fever. Dr Wierzbowska, whom we could always rely on, arranged a place in the hospital on Wolska street.

I was supposed to take her there. But when I left home it turned out to be too late. I had no chance of getting to Wolska street and returning to Miodowa street before the curfew. So I decided to take her for the night to my place on Miodowa street. Marysia was staying at Leszno street and I was alone, and I was not afraid of scarlet fever.

We went to Miodowa street. I went to my room with the child and discovered that the light didn't work. Total darkness. In one of the neighbouring rooms lived an electrician.

"Wait here for a moment, Jasia," I said, "I am going to fetch someone who will repair the light."

After a little while the light went on again. On the bed beneath the picture of Our Lady knelt a small, fair-haired girl, her hands clasped together, saying a prayer.

Jasia survived the whole of the Warsaw Uprising at Janina's. Afterwards they left Warsaw together, for Piaseczno, I think.

Throughout the whole of this period I used to visit her every week and I was certain that the child didn't remember anything about her origins. After all she was so small. While at Janina's she started going to school at the convent and she enjoyed it there.

After the liberation, Janina, who was an exceptionally honest person, felt that it was her duty to tell the child the truth. She didn't know whether anybody from her family or her guardians had survived the Uprising. She wanted to keep the child with her, but for her to know who she was.

You can imagine her astonishment when after the first sentence little Jasia asked: "So auntie knew my real name all along?"

To deliver children to Father Boduen's foundlings home, we would take them to a rendezvous in the entrance to a particular building at a prearranged time. They would be taken from there by a navy-blue policeman who worked with us, who would deliver them to the home.

In this way Irenka was taken there. Her mother worked as a servant and her father died a soldier's death in the ghetto. The child was all her mother had left.

Irenka's mother went to see her. After arranging it with Dr Wierzbowska, I stood with her mother one day on the staircase of the house opposite the foundlings home. The figure of a woman holding in her arms a little girl with a pink ribbon in her hair appeared in the window.

That is all I remember about the children. But there were other difficult problems.

Chapter Nineteen

❖ ❖ ❖ ❖ ❖

ADULTS IN HIDING

There were the problems of those who were locked up, or separated from their loved ones, who had no chance of seeing their husbands, wives and children, and sometimes did not even have news of them, as they were often lodged somewhere in the countryside or in monasteries. I don't remember the exact dates. These things all took place in 1943 and 1944.

Dr R. was able to go out and walk about the town. I used to meet him in the street to give him money. He wanted desperately to get the address of his wife from me. I didn't give it to him, but he got it from somewhere else. He told me about it triumphantly at one of our meetings. I begged him not to go there, saying that he shouldn't expose her to risk. He didn't listen to me. But he didn't get there either. He was caught in a round-up and died in the Pawiak prison. For a few months afterwards I continued passing on greetings to his wife. She complained that her husband had stopped writing, and in the end I had to tell her the truth, because she had started to suspect and to threaten that she would go to his house to look for him. She threw herself at me and started to hit me . . .

On Marszalkowska street I met Dr W. He was a doctor from our hospital. Both he and his wife looked perfectly Aryan and spoke faultless Polish. They had found lodgings without any difficulty, in which they lived together with their five-year-old son. They didn't at that time need any financial help, so I hadn't had any contact with them before that accidental meeting.

The strict rules of the underground ordered that friends you bumped into in the street should be passed by without a smile or any sign of recognition. So I was very surprised when this composed, quiet man almost threw himself at me.

"What good luck! What good luck!" he repeated agitatedly.

I managed to calm his emotional outburst. I suggested we go to a café.

He told me that they had found themselves in a terrible situation. They had been recognized by some friends of his landlords. By an unfortunate coincidence, one of these people had been a patient of his or his wife's before the war. It wasn't, however, a question of blackmail. The landlords had simply become scared by the sudden realization that they were putting up a Jewish family, and suggested that they move out as soon as possible, especially as an outsider already knew about them. It turned out that this was the second time this had happened. They now had a steadily diminishing amount of money and a child they didn't want to be separated from.

Prior to our chance meeting his wife had a nervous breakdown. She became very depressed. He could not see any way out. They considered a suicide pact. In fact, they did more than just think about it. They made preparations for it.

They prepared three portions of poison. They thought that the child didn't understand. The child was to drink the first portion. While holding the cup in his hand the child started to shout desperately.

"Mamma, I don't want it! I want to live!" And he threw down the cup. His mother picked up the child and hugged him to her. She burst into tears.

They gave up the idea of the final solution.

They started to look for help.

Our meeting turned out to be that help.

Once again Dr Skonieczny came to our aid.

Dr W. got a job as a porter in a doctor's surgery on the Aleje Jerozolimskie, where Dr Skonieczny was one of the partners. A small room in the entrance of the building, something like a prewar porter's lodge, went along with the job. Dr W. and his family lived there until the Warsaw Uprising, survived the war, and afterwards emigrated to Sweden.

That episode ended happily.

Mrs Goldman, a secretary from our hospital, lived with her beautiful daughter Noemi. They were distant relatives of mine, and I visited them quite often. Noemi, a typical Jewish beauty, shouldn't have gone out into the street. One day she peroxided her hair and convinced herself that it would be safe for her to go out. She couldn't bear being shut up. She wouldn't listen to our pleas and explanations. She went out of the house . . . and she didn't come back. Her mother stayed on there on her own. She survived the war.

My old aunt, in fact my aunt's mother, lived with her old housekeeper. I kept looking for a better place for her, but I couldn't find one. One day I was informed that she was out on the street. Through some unfortunate accident, the information reached me a day late. I didn't find her where we were supposed to have met. Only after the war did I find that she had met a friend of her son's, Eugeniusz Szwankowski, who was later to become a well-known architect. He found a place for her in the hospital, where she died of natural causes. But at the time I thought that she had died like the others.

She was the last living member of my family.

The news from Majdanek also came too late. I heard about it from Professor Michalowicz's wife, who had been there visiting her husband. It was a message from my brother-in-law, Mietek, his wife and the Ferszt family, an administrator and laboratory assistant from the hospital on Sliska street. We managed to bribe a Ukrainian, who said that he would try to buy them out. We were too late. They had died a few days earlier.

*　　*　　*

There were also problems that I had to deal with because of my "profession". After all, in my previous life I had been a doctor.

There was the problem of medical equipment and dressings which we had to send into the forest. That was usually straightforward, but there was one exceptional case, when a girl in the forest became pregnant, in January 1944. I had to go to the forest and perform the abortion. But before that I had to get hold of the right instruments. Although I obtained the instruments, I was unable to perform the operation. After all, I was only a junior paediatrician. In Warsaw I had a friend from Medical School who was two years senior to me. He said that he knew how to do it. He went and did the operation. After a few weeks it transpired that the pregnancy was progressing normally. The girl's husband died in battle, and she was brought to Warsaw. She was hidden in the house of a tram worker or railway worker, somewhere on Rakowiecka street, and survived there until the Uprising. She delivered a healthy boy in a makeshift delivery room in a cellar on Hoza street, and left Warsaw with her infant when it was only a few days old. They survived, living with a farmer near Warsaw.

*   *   *

It was already the spring of 1944. We knew that we only had to last out a little longer. It was then that all the most difficult things started. The fighters and the messenger girls were a group of young people, some of them very young. Although at times things were very bad and extremely hard, as long as we weren't dying of hunger, and as long as we could forget about fear at home in the evenings, and didn't have to listen out all the time for footsteps on the stairs, life blossomed.

People fell in love despite everything that was going on around them. Couples met and fell in love – Antek with Celina, Kazik with Irka and Marysia with Zygmunt.

And me? I didn't go into mourning after Stefan's death. It

was as if something within me had burnt out, and I couldn't, nor did I wish to, think about the fact that he had gone there in that train, which was supposed to have taken him to freedom, but took him instead to the gas chambers. Something within me died. It seemed as though forever.

It was about then that I started seeing Bernard. No, I didn't love him.

My love, after all, had gone away in the prison lorry that took him from the Polish Hotel. But I had a lot of respect and admiration for Bernard. He was old. In any case to me he seemed terribly old. But he wanted us very much to be together. He was very unhappy in his hiding place beneath the floor, where I used to go and see him. His conditions there were fairly good, he had a bed and a table, but all the same, he was shut up. And those who were shut up and lonely were always the most unhappy.

In fact, Bernard did go out at times. He had "good" looks, but he spoke Polish poorly, and he was afraid. He went out only when it was necessary, to attend important meetings, or "high level" conferences; he even came to Miodowa street for some meetings, but most of the time he just sat in his shelter. One day, when he had got a bit merry, he broke his leg. He had to lie on his bed under the floor, and I used to climb down a ladder to him. He spent six long weeks with his leg in plaster.

It started about then. It was as though it didn't make any difference to me, because if Stefan wasn't there any longer, and he so wanted us to be together, I thought to myself, well, why not? What difference does it make to me? Because I never thought seriously that there would be something after the war. Besides, even if there were, it wouldn't be the same.

By this time I already felt very old. Or at least it seemed to me that I had already experienced everything good, and everything important in life, so that everything that happened to me now was unimportant.

But it turned out to be otherwise, that there were still hard and difficult times ahead, both for me and for others.

The first problems were my own. I was pregnant, or so it seemed to me, as I had all sorts of symptoms, and as though that were not enough, I had an attack of appendicitis. I lay in bed on Miodowa street, feeling terrible.

Doctor Margolis contacted Dr Marek Landsberg, who came to see me.

I got a shock when I saw him, and let myself down. Because this was the man whose wife we had helped to die in the hospital . . .

I had to tell him all about it. It was like an awkward scene, as though from a kitsch film. I lay in bed with my appendicitis, and he knelt by the bed, kissing my hands, and said that now he could die in peace. And then he left.

The appendicitis got better with cold compresses. Fortunately it didn't recur until 1946, when an operation was no longer a problem.

But the second problem remained. I had to find a way out. I don't remember who gave me the address of a "trusted" doctor, who was prepared to do the operation for a large sum, which I had to ask for. It was not nice at all. And the very idea was not very nice either. The doctor was skilful, but terribly vulgar. Obviously he did the operation without anaesthetic, and it was a terrible experience for me. The worst thing, however, was that because I had had to get some extra money, Bernard found out about it, and we had an awful row.

And what was I to tell him? Did I have to explain to him that we lived in times in which children didn't have the right to be born, because they should be born only for life, and not for death? Did I have to burden him as well with what I felt myself? It was bad enough that I had to talk about it several times, and that I had to take three other young girls for the same operation, each of whom might, as a consequence, never be able to have children. Especially as I couldn't guarantee them anything except the operation itself. There were no facilities for convalescence.

But that was the way it had to be. Because who knew better than I that children had no right to be born?

I had promised myself that I would not allow it to happen. Because it seemed to me, and it still seems to me, that everything is better than the loss of a child, a living child.

I had to be present at each operation. I had to hold the girls by the hand and make sure that they didn't scream. I did not like it at all, I detest the thought to this day, but that was the way it had to be. We were involved in some cunning two-way blackmail with this doctor. He blackmailed me, saying that he knew who I was bringing, and raised his fees accordingly, and I blackmailed him with the fact that he was carrying out illegal operations. It was disgusting!

At times I used to wonder why everything had suddenly started to happen this last spring. After all, there had been hiding places, shelters with young men and girls together before . . .

Maybe these people, so mortally tired, sought oblivion in love, or maybe they just stopped being careful, because it didn't matter to them any more. Why, I don't know, but that is what happened.

It was a very difficult time for me. I had no one with whom I could talk about it. Partly perhaps because of "professional confidence", although that is not quite true because for every operation I had to get money from somewhere, and partly because I had nobody whom I could burden with my own unimportant experiences.

I found help. From the most unexpected quarter.

Celina and Antek were very much in love. It was not a war-time romance, but the sort of love that is for life. They had conceived their first child. Celina, the hard masculine Celina, broke down. Just like everybody else. Like any other girl.

She came to see me – no, in fact, I went to visit her, and sat with her while she cried. She cried like someone who has forgotten what tears are.

I started to talk. I told her why it had to be like this.

I told her about the infant who had been suffocated by a pillow, and about the one who died, God knows why, and was found dead in the morning, and about a third child, which I hadn't been able to save from a simple chest infection.

Somehow I managed to quieten her down, or rather to convince her. Later on, when she had the operation in the doctor's surgery, I had to hold her by the hand, but I didn't have to tell her not to scream. Because this was Celina, strong and hard. I went to see her daily for the first few days. That, I think, is when our "womanly" friendship started.

In the end I told her about everything. How I was no longer able to cope, and how I was losing my strength. Because whatever we seemed to do – all of the everyday things, like giving people money, distributing underground bulletins, saving those who were "burned" – it was all nothing. At most it was something that might scare us. But the incessant involvement in people's misfortunes was more than I could bear. Celina helped me. Just by understanding and by being with me. But I didn't know that the worst was yet to come.

But it came.

I don't know, perhaps I should have refused. After all it wasn't a job for a doctor. Except that no one understood this. There was no other doctor among us at that time. And so I didn't have anyone to talk to, to tell that I would rather die than do this. It would have been easier to die myself than to carry out euthanasia on someone who was mentally ill.

She used to run out into the street and shout in Yiddish.

She posed a mortal threat for the landlords and for the half a dozen or so young people hiding in the house, among them her own daughter.

But I couldn't do it!

But I did it. At the request of her daughter.

But I don't want to write any more. Not a sentence more. About anything.

TO OUR FRIENDS ACROSS THE SEA

We know, brother –
A storm rends the night, trees rustle –
You bury your face in your hands,
Ghosts beat at your windows and doors,
All your loved ones have perished –
You alone survive.

We know –
The wine in your trembling hand
Stains the white table-cloth red
Thus arrives your dead sweetheart's letter
Full of that autumn's blood.

We know –
You keep vigil at night by the radio:
And hear only waves breaking with an empty moan.
But you persist maniacally, hoping
"Maybe somehow, somewhere, they are still alive?"

Then –
You tear your own heart to pieces
And send them, bleeding, to your Polish home,
In scores of letters, scores of white, trembling letters.

We know, O Friend!
We know –
Your heart is joining us across the sea
To burn with ours on the funeral pyre.

Hear us –
Our last stronghold is a smoking ruin,
But if one beating heart is saved,
In that one heart still beat the hearts of millions,
The eternal flame burns, the spirit lives!
Above the ghetto's ruins,
Above Treblinka and Aleje Szucha,
Above the chimneys of the death-chambers
Rises the sacrificial smoke of that spirit!

Do not weep, brother –
Do not bury your face in your hands.
Believe us, death is not that hard,
Knowing that our funeral pyre
Will become freedom's burning dawn!

ADINA BLADY SZWAJGER
(1943)

❖ ❖ ❖ ❖ ❖

INSTEAD OF AN EPILOGUE

When I finished the last page of my memoirs, I went back to the beginning. I read them through – and suddenly realized that something was wrong.

I had wanted to bear witness to the true events of those times, but I had done it very awkwardly.

Over the last forty-five years, the world has changed, new generations have grown up, and everything that happened has faded in the mists of history, or even prehistory.

Everything has changed – even the streets I wrote about are no longer on the map of contemporary Warsaw. So much of what I wrote has ceased to be clear and comprehensible. Only for one man here in Poland,* and for a few dozen – maybe a few score – around the world, my words are clear, and tell of something we know about.

But those are not the important ones. We have crossed the barrier of shadows, and one by one we are leaving. The young are left behind. And it would be a good thing if something of those years remained for them. And so we need to explain, not just to reminisce. I don't know whether I am able to. I am not a professional writer, or a chronicler. But I must try – try to add a bit of history to what I remember.

*   *   *

The first major exterminations in the Warsaw ghetto lasted from 22 July 1942 until 8 August 1942. Six weeks. In the last

* Marek Edelman.

four days there was the final selection from the square formed by four streets – Mila street, Zamenhofa street, Gesia street and Smocza street – the so-called "melting pot". All those left alive were herded into this area, and the only people who could leave were those who had received "life tickets", little white cards with a stamp, which they had to pin to their clothes. I don't know who used to give out these cards to workers in their workshops, but the cards for the staff of the Jewish Community, the hospital, etc. were given to the *Judenrat** by the Germans, so that the Jews themselves could choose those who were to survive.

In our hospital, Dr Braude-Heller, the Head Doctor, had to give them out. She didn't want to do it, and we almost had to force her to. Supposedly all of those with tickets would be able to get out of the "melting pot", but it all seemed to get mixed up. The Germans counted people in fours as they went out, and at a given moment said: "Stop!" All of those left, whether they had tickets or not, went to the wagons. But in any case there were many "illegals", that is, those without work, in the crowd, and a few children were carried out in bundles, in sacks of potatoes, in suitcases, etc.

Altogether there were a little more than the official 40,000 left – perhaps 50,000?

The lives of those who had been saved for the moment did not resemble normal life.

Above all, no one could stay in his own house. People were billeted near their workplaces; only the streets on which there were factories or offices or the hospital were inhabited, and the rest of the ghetto was "dead ground". But even those inhabited streets were empty during the day. From dawn until dusk it was illegal to move about on the streets. The Germans shot on sight anyone who wandered on to the streets. After all, those who were still alive were workers, and so they should be working during the day, not wandering in the streets. And so the streets were empty. Except that

* *Judenrat*: the Council of Jewish elders who administered the ghetto.

from time to time a figure, wrapped in rags, would sneak along beneath the walls. Everyone had to exchange their ration cards in the shops. A half a loaf of bread for four days, and a few hundred grams of jam or synthetic honey. To buy a few potatoes or some fat, they had to search out other sources.

Sometimes there would be a cart of "stinkers", terribly smelly fish that we used to make soup from. There was also a "horse butcher's stall", except that it didn't sell meat, only blood. The blood would be scalded with boiling water, and when it clotted it would be cut into small pieces and steamed. It resembled lung. In the evening the dark streets used to fill up a little. No one went out who didn't have to, but people still had to get some money to live on. A loaf of bread on the black market cost fifteen zlotys. Where did the black market come from? Well, of course – from smuggling. How? There were two ways. Things thrown over the wall, and things brought in by the "outworkers" – those who worked outside. The smugglers, those from the Aryan side, earned a lot of money. It was a job for bloodsuckers, and risky, so it had to be profitable. In the ghetto those who used to take deliveries from outside, but above all the "outworkers", used to earn a lot.

The "outworkers" were those Jews who used to go out under guard to work in factories on the Aryan side, that is, beyond the walls. At work they might be able to buy bread, potatoes, sometimes a piece of meat smuggled from the villages, and to bring it into the ghetto. Obviously they too had to pay above the odds, because the salesmen who used to come to where the Jews worked risked a few strokes of the whip, or if the guards were in a bad mood, even a bullet. And so it had to be profitable!

Before a smuggled piece of bread or a kilo of potatoes could reach the customer, several intermediaries would have earned their money on it: the smugglers on both sides of the wall, or the "outworkers", and the "wholesalers" (those who would buy five kilos of potatoes at a time, or a few loaves of bread,

sometimes a kilo of sugar, flour, cereals or even a few grams of lard).

And the question arises: where did people get the money for these purchases? Well, of course, smuggling went on in both directions. Everything that people could do without would be sold – clothes, trinkets – and through the outworkers this would end up on the Aryan side, where the same blood-suckers would line their pockets as traders in goods "from the Jews", buying for a few groszy the remnants of the worldly goods of those sentenced to death.

Those who worked in the hospital lived in one block of rented apartments at 6 Gesia street, on the same street as the hospital. In our flat on the third floor eleven people lived in three rooms with a kitchen. There were my closest friends from the hospital, and a few people from their families – Dr Margolis and her daughter, Dr Hela Keilson and her parents, Marek and I. Apart from us, Stasia (Ryfka) and her young man, Welwl Rozowski, and also Alik Zarchi, a boy who was the younger brother of a friend from Medical School, who had died together with her parents in the first wave of exterminations. I managed to send this boy over to the Aryan side, where his parents had left their furniture and money with some friends. I later found out that these people had let him down completely. This boy roamed the streets until eventually he ended up back in the ghetto, where he died . . .

We lived like all the others, except that we didn't have anything to sell. Except that Dola Keilson and Marysia (Bronka Feinmesser), still had passes in the beginning, and sometimes would bring us food, which we used to sell for bread. After that, until November, Dr Skonieczny, the Dean of the Hospital, came a few times, but some time at the beginning of November they took away his pass as well.

We obtained money by exchanging currency, that is, five-rouble coins, which I used to sell on behalf of my aunt. One coin used to bring fifty zlotys, enough for three loaves of bread. I learnt to divide these loaves up so that the portions would be exactly equal . . . To this day I have the marks on

the index finger of my right hand from this cutting. Ryfka, who didn't work, used to cook for us. In fact with her organization and self-control she used to "keep house" for us.

We didn't feel cramped. Everyone had a place to lie down, and in the kitchen we could heat water and wash, so we lived in "luxury".

In this interval of a few months between the end of the first wave of exterminations, and the beginning of the second in January, there arose an organization called ZOB – the Jewish Fighting Organization. Marek was the second in command, and Welwl was a fighter. From the very beginning it became clear that they made the rules, and we had to listen – and to worry about them. Because they were always out of the house with their vital affairs, and we were scared to death that they might not come back. After all, on the streets the German soldiers used to shoot at people as they would at sparrows.

People used to come to our flat. Abrasza Blum and others. Sometimes they would stay for the night. Then, we used to talk and to read. Sometimes we would forget about the terror. Because despite the terror the atmosphere in our house was probably better than elsewhere. When you are thinking about fighting it is different from just being scared of death or looking for help.

On the whole, people in the ghetto were divided into that handful which was preparing for armed resistance, those who were no longer counting on anything (and these were the most numerous) and those who were looking for a way of saving themselves and their families. Those who had friends on the Aryan side, or who had a lot of money, looked for a way of getting out of the ghetto; others built themselves hideouts in cellars, and thought they would survive there. But there were very few of these; the majority thought about hiding on the Aryan side.

To do that required a few very genuine friends, and lots of money. First you had to pay the foreman of the outworkers, that is, the man who took people out to work on the Aryan side, to let you go out with the work parties. That involved large sums, because they had to bribe the gendarmes at the *Wache*. The bribed gendarmes didn't check the papers of those going out very carefully. Once through the gate, you had skilfully to remove the armband with the Star of David from your sleeve, and to mix with the crowd. But it wasn't that easy, because around the gate swarmed a crowd of those who were looking for the opportunity to buy something cheap from the outworkers, and extortionists – blackmailers who were looking for easy pickings, or a reward from the Germans for taking a Jew to the police. It often happened that people who had managed to pass through the gate were fleeced of everything by the time they got past the wall, and so had no way out – they had to return to the ghetto to wait for death. Without money there was no chance for them on the Aryan side.

But even with money it was difficult.

The whole miserable existence of those who escaped from the ghetto can be summed up in one word – terror.

Not many people had true friends on the other side who could help them immediately in those worst first few hours, when they had to change their skin. Not only to wash from themselves the dirt of their miserable pallet, but to wipe from their faces the picture of dread and despair. To become as other people walking normally along the street, and not to sneak along under the walls of the buildings, not to run away at the sight of a German, but to hide at the sight of a familiar face from the past. Because you never knew who this "acquaintance" might be now, with whom in ancient times you might have spoken in the street, or in a café, as "one person with another". He might still be someone who wished to hold out his hand in help – there were those as well. He could be decent enough to pass his unseeing eyes over a once familiar face, which meant: I don't know you, I don't want to know that you are here, and I won't tell anybody.

But there were those as well who would come up to you and say: "Come on, you Jew," and take you straight to the Germans, or those who would say: "Pay for my silence," and take the shirt from your back.

All of these things happened and caused terror.

Terror in the streets, and terror at home. In the shelters for which we had paid with everything which we had been able to save, because those who decided to let some corner to a Jew risked their lives. They had to get something in return. Some were satisfied with the modest maintenance which was their due. "Servicing" a hidden lodger required extra shopping, sometimes in distant shops so as not to awaken suspicion, extra difficulties with washing, cleaning, avoiding any contact with neighbours, even avoiding leaving one's house for any period, so that there wouldn't be any signs of life in a supposedly empty house. These conditions prevented any other paid employment and such landlords had to have something to live on.

Many people believed that Jews were "made of money" and that their compensation for the difficulty and risk should be the provision of luxury! These people were doubly dangerous. When the money ran out there would be no mercy.

"On the street with you, no one is going to take risks for nothing!"

And besides that there were curious neighbours, wondering who had moved in with "those on the third floor" and whispering that "that cousin from the country looks very Jewish". These whispers led either to blackmail, or to a straightforward decision by the inhabitants of the house to "tell that Jewess to go, because we too have children, and we're not going to risk our lives". No amount of good will on the part of the hosts would help. A new shelter had to be found. The safest people of all – the irony of fate – were those who, because of their typically Jewish looks, were unable to go out into the street or even to move about the house. Hidden in ingenious hiding places, in closed cages, not coming up to the windows, walking about in their socks, or lying all day on the bed – as long as they did not go mad, and as long as their money lasted – had the chance of surviving in hiding.

Those with "good" looks were supposedly the lucky ones. They were able to walk in the street, to buy all the necessary things, a few of them could even work. But in reality they were threatened at every moment. Above all, they were subjected to the same terror as all the inhabitants of Warsaw. Nobody, Pole or Jew, leaving home knew whether he would come back. At any moment it could turn out that the prison lorries would drive up to the street, the exit to the street would be closed off, and all the passers-by would be taken into the vans, to the prisons on Skaryszewska street or Gesiowka street, to be sent as forced labour to Germany. But it could also be the path to Pawiak, to the prison where the way out was either summary execution or the camps. This happened especially after an act of sabotage by the underground – the resistance movement.

Except that there were certain differences. A Pole who was caught in an ordinary round-up, the sort that was for forced labour, as long as he had a good *Ausweis* – a certificate of employment – or money to bribe the gendarme, could come out in one piece. A Jew who was caught, especially a man, had almost no chance. His false papers were usually easy to check. Besides that, before being sent to Germany, there was a medical examination. In the Pawiak and Gesia prisons there were prisoner-doctors who consciously failed to recognize Jews. But there were also those who conscientiously used to point out any who were circumcised – and those were summarily executed.

Papers were important, very important, so as not to be caught straight away during an incidental identity check, which could happen anywhere – in the street, in the shops, in the trams. These false *Kennkarten* – proof of identity, which all Poles had to have – were sometimes obtained from the underground organizations, and sometimes bought from forgers, who made this a very profitable occupation for themselves. Very few people had really "good" papers. They were those who had managed to obtain the real birth certificates of dead people, and on that basis had made themselves out real identity cards, and real registration documents. Providing papers to those who were in hiding was one of our most important duties as courier girls for ZOB.

A danger one hundred times greater than being accidentally caught in a round-up were the "extortionists" – blackmailers who had a nose for "smelling out" a Jew in a crowd, going up to him and demanding that he pay them. And if he didn't have any money – well, then the Germans used to pay for Jews delivered to them.

How the extortionists used to get hold of the addresses of Jews who were in hiding we will never know. But they used to come to the flats and take everything from people – right down to their wedding rings. The arrival of extortionists at a flat was the ultimate disaster, as after the first plundering there would come another, until the moment when the helpless people, stripped of everything, were handed over into the hands of the "appropriate authorities".

And so the arrival of blackmailers – if one managed to get rid of them on that occasion – meant an immediate change of lodgings, of papers, and of registration. This was called the "burning" of a place – because it really was a conflagration.

The life of these supposedly saved people really was one long nightmare. And so no wonder that so many people were taken in by the terrible plan of the "Hotel Poland".

This plan arose because theoretically Jews who were citizens of neutral countries were not supposed to be exterminated. When the world eventually started to believe in what was going on, families abroad started to send their relatives in Poland certificates of citizenship, usually for South American countries. But these documents arrived too late; those they were addressed to had died long before. And then the Germans fell upon the diabolical idea of selling these papers through the agency of the Jewish Gestapo to Jews who were still alive and in hiding. These "foreign nationals" were to leave Poland officially, to go initially to Switzerland, and then to the countries they belonged to. The first transport really did go to a camp at Vitell in Switzerland, and letters started to come from there. But we didn't find out that the rest shared the fate of those Jews left behind in Poland until after a small group of real citizens of the United States and, I think, of Portugal did in fact arrive where they were supposed to.

But as I have already written, we didn't know about that. When the news about the "second intake" of foreigners was received – and these documents were sold for enormous sums – many people who were mortally tired by their life on the volcano were taken in and voluntarily presented themselves for the voyage, buying other people's papers.

These "foreign nationals" were brought together in Warsaw in the "Hotel Poland" on Dluga street, and after a few days of supposedly good treatment, they were taken off to Auschwitz.

That is what life looked like for those who escaped the ghetto to the Aryan side. No, I haven't forgotten about anything.

Not about Zegota.

Or about the good will of many ordinary people.

Or about the "Righteous among nations".*

Or those who, fully aware of what they were doing, risked their lives to save people who were no longer protected by any sort of law.

There was, in any case, no law for anybody in those times of contempt. I remember all those who knew that we are all of one earth, that "He who saves a man saves the whole world." In my memoirs they take up more room than the bad people, because I remember them better, and will remember them always, whereas the others have remained without a name, and deserve to be forgotten. Constantly I reminisce

---

* "Righteous among nations": Poles who helped the Jews during the Holocaust.

about those who were close to me, and are closest to me to this day.

No amount of love or respect would ever be enough to repay Marysia Sawicka, who "covered" the flat in which two members of the staff of ZOB and several fighters found shelter, and who will always be our closest friend. We won't forget her sister, Anna Wechalska who is no longer alive. We won't forget, nor will we be able to repay our gratitude to, the late Henryk Wolinski (Waclaw), the representative of the government in exile's Commission, and Director of its Jewish Department, for his care and friendship. Or Professor Prokopowicz (Wierzbowska) for her help in saving so many children, Professor Kacprzak for his help in saving academics, and many others . . .

And there were many others. Many died, and probably everyone who was saved has someone whom he remembers with respect and love.

But the street had a cruel face. Foreign, indifferent, but sometimes smiling maliciously.

The best understood this – the resistance used to pass sentence on extortionists, provocateurs and traitors. But there were also other underground groups – partisans who used to attack Jewish fighters in the forests after they had left the ghetto. Many people were killed. Receiving our safe conduct from the High Command of the Home Army – which recognized these Jewish fighters as part of that army – was so long drawn out that we had to take our people from the forest.

People used to feed the children who begged – but it did happen that sometimes people delivered these children straight into the hands of the Germans – to their deaths. It was very difficult to help them.

Czeslaw Milosz's poem "Campo dei Fiori" was distributed in the underground press.

Around the "Square of Flowers", while Giordano Bruno was being burnt at the stake, the mob on the street was laughing and dancing.

In Warsaw, on Krasinski square, outside the walls of a

burning ghetto in that awful Easter of 1943 the merry-go-round went round and jolly music played. And people enjoyed themselves.

And that is why the part of my memoirs dealing with the Ghetto Uprising is called "Campo dei Fiori".

Because I stood by that merry-go-round, I looked at what was going on behind the walls and I looked at those who were on the merry-go-round.

And I too was smiling.

But I never want to smile like that again.

Someone asked me: "What was the reaction of those people on Krasinski square?" And also: "What could you see?" And I of course don't know. Because I had eyes that were dry, but blind. I saw my house burning – right behind the walls – but that wasn't the first day. I heard the shots, the explosions, but where? When? There? Or behind the wall on Muranowska street? It is all like one day and one picture, one awful noise of houses collapsing in flames, and shooting – one picture of hell.

I only know that people said afterwards that there were two standards – the white and red, and the Star of David. And there was a sign "For our freedom and yours", but I didn't see it.

And the people? On Krasinski Square, and on the streets generally? For me they all had one face, an empty one. Because it was all far away. Behind the wall. It just did not concern them. In the same way we are not really concerned about children dying from hunger in Biafra, Ethiopia or in India.

But I remember the laughter of children. Because they were playing, and going round on the merry-go-round. And the music was playing.

And other questions have been asked.

For example: why, when we were parting under the wall, did Michal Klepfisz say something about Lodzia and Irenka? Because they were his wife and daughter. Maybe he knew that he wouldn't return? I don't know. But they survived.

And also: what happened on 10 May 1943 – why were there lorries on Prosta street? I thought that everyone knew about this. That Kazik went with the sewermen through the sewers to the ghetto, and led out the survivors of the staff and the fighters. They came out of the exit on Prosta street during the day, fully armed, and got into the lorries, which were waiting for them, and drove off into the forest.

And Krzaczek was a young man from the Polish underground, I think from AL (the People's Army), who was a messenger between us and those who were helping. He had arranged these lorries. The sewermen were the worst extortionists, but they were threatened that if they betrayed anyone, they would be sentenced by the underground. And so they went.

And one other question: what were the tragi-comic moments?

Yes, this was lost in the memoirs. Because even in the greatest tragedies, there is often something to laugh about, for example once when we were living on Miodowa street, Antek (Icchak Cukierman) came for the night. I don't remember why, it doesn't matter. It happened quite often. He slept on a mattress on the floor.

At seven o'clock, there was a sudden knock at the door. We thought for a moment – and put the mattress under the bed. Marysia got up and put on her dressing gown, and Antek jumped into the bed in her place, by the wall; his head under the pillow, the duvet over him, with me lying next to him as though alone.

Mr Trediakowski came in, the man who provided papers. He was a cheerful and trustworthy man. But it is always better to know less. He sat by the table, Marysia with him, and I lay on the bed – and we talked. And he suddenly started to laugh. He was unable to control himself. We looked at him, and he said to me: "Haven't your legs grown, hey?" Because Antek was tall, and his enormous feet in their stockings stuck out from the end of the bedclothes.

And once in Miedzylesie, during a false alarm, Celek

jumped out of a window half naked – and fell into the raspberries.

*　　*　　*

And so I understand that after forty-five years I have been unable to write an "account" of those years, only my own, fragmented, incomplete and very personal memoirs.

But I wanted people to know in the future that ZOB was not only the Ghetto Uprising, and that even if only through a few survivors, it was also what came afterwards.

A fight for humanity.

For forty years after the war I was a doctor. I believe, I really believe, that one is a doctor in order to save life, anywhere and at any time.

For forty years I have never departed from this view.

But somewhere underneath I thought that I had no right to carry out my profession. After all, one does not start one's work as a doctor by leading people not to life but to death.

And I have lived with this knowledge to this day.

And it does not help me that I know that it was all in order to save people's lives, that it was all necessary. But along the way something was not as it should have been.

Maybe it was too heavy a burden for the rest of my life?

❖ ❖ ❖ ❖ ❖

AFTERWORD

I will now address a general question raised by my publishers and others who read the manuscript – perhaps the most serious criticism of all: that my story doesn't seem to "have an end". There was, of course, the Warsaw Uprising, and yet there is nothing about what happened to all of us at that time, and how we managed to survive until the end of the war. There is a quick answer to that. These are the memories of a courier girl from ZOB, and my role and my work with and among these people in fact ended with the outbreak of the Uprising.

But that wouldn't be a complete answer.

And so I will include in this afterword a few reminiscences about the final period, from August 1944 to January 1945.

On 1 August 1944, I was alone in my flat on Miodowa street. Zosia and Joanna had gone out as they had something to arrange in Ochota. The atmosphere in town was expectant and uncertain. Once again, as had happened two days before, people were waiting for "W hour" (the codename for the Uprising), but for reasons unknown to us the alert was called off.

And so there was suspense – when would it be? Today?

At five o'clock I heard shots. I ran out on to the stairs. I will never forget that moment. Somebody was running down the stairs – a Polish officer!! In the uniform of the Carpathian Brigade!* Everybody cried, and I cried with them. There was a commotion in the basement. I went downstairs. They

---

* Carpathian Brigade: the equivalent of the Black Watch.

were organizing a field hospital. I went up to the commander, a Major "Pobog", whose surname I don't remember. I introduced myself. I said who I was and was immediately accepted as one of the hospital staff. It had turned out that of those who were supposed to have come to work in the hospital almost no one had managed to get there. Apart from myself, two other doctors appeared, both of them Jewish. They were Dr Ludwig Koenigstein "Rakieta" (Rocket), the son of an eminent Warsaw ENT surgeon, himself an ENT surgeon, and Dr Boleslaw Krzywonos, whose real surname I don't remember. Both were with their wives, and lived near the hospital. (Their wives found work there as nurses). Dr Koenigstein also had his five-year-old son with him.

For the moment there was little to do. I went out into the street. By the gate stood a young man in civilian clothes. We started to talk. He introduced himself as the "Prefect" of North Warsaw – Wik Slawski. He didn't yet have an office. I offered him our room on the first floor. In return, on discovering that I was a paediatrician, he appointed me the paediatrician to the Prefecture, which of course, at the time of the Uprising, was completely nonsensical. Once again I had to watch helplessly as infants for whom I could do nothing died. We had nothing, neither milk nor medicines. Not even water. But I write about this because Wik Slawski – Wladyslaw Swidowski – was later to become my husband.

The first days of the Uprising passed in euphoria. The Old Town was ours, and the *Wehrmacht* warehouses on Stawki street were broken into and provided us with tinned food, wine and German uniforms. (The resistance, who up till now had mostly worn civilian clothes with red and white armbands, now dressed in grey-green camouflage combat jackets and helmets.) We did not know what was going on in other areas. There were rumours that "Cedergren", the telephone exchange in the town centre, had been captured. We knew nothing about the massacre in Wola, or about the execution of the doctors in the hospital on Plocka street. Our hospital quickly filled up with wounded.

I worked hard, like everyone else, but I was very worried about our people in Leszno, and about Zosia and Joanna, who had stayed somewhere in Warsaw. On the third day the girls found their way home. Both of them found work in the hospital. Joanna was a qualified nurse, and Zosia an "apprentice".

Now we were all together, and together we feared for our friends. They joined us the next day. Marek, Antek and Celina, Marysia and Zygmunt, and Julek, Zosia's boyfriend. The others stayed in Leszno. The Germans rounded them up and we did not find the survivors until after the war. Our men reported to the commander of a unit which was stationed on the same yard. They were not accepted. There was no need for a unit of Jewish fighters. So they went to AL, where they were accepted. They were billeted not far away, beyond Krasinski square in the ruins of the old bazaar on Swietojerska street. Zosia wanted to be with Julek. She went to join them. Joanna and I stayed, we couldn't leave the hospital by then.

So much has been written about the Warsaw Uprising that there is no point in repeating stories about the greatness and nightmare of those sixty-three days. I saw it all. The wounded and the dying, the bombers and the snipers, the shooting of civilians, ten- to twelve-year-old boys maintaining communications between different areas through the sewers, the lack of light and water, doctors operating by candlelight, not interrupting the operation when the windows in the operating theatre were blasted out. Joanna and I used to go out to places which had been bombed and where people had to be pulled out of the rubble. I remember one such trip when a three-tonner landed on the Polish Bank on Bielanska street. A dressing station was buried under the rubble. Above the cellar housing the dressing station there hung an enormous concrete block, which looked as though it was going to collapse. We pulled two wounded nurses and three bodies out of there.

About the third week of the Uprising a Canadian aeroplane

shot down by the Germans fell on to our house. We saw the charred bodies of the airmen who had come to help Warsaw. A few days later a heavy shell struck the house and destroyed part of the hospital. The commander, "Pobog", was killed. One day Dr Koenigstein ("Rakieta") went out for a moment into the hospital courtyard, and never came back. After the war he was dug out from that courtyard, but how he had died we never found out. We also lost Dr Krzywonos. Apparently he was traced after the war, but I don't know where. Joanna and I and a group of "apprentice" nurses were left alone with forty wounded. The end of the Old Town was near. That was when we experienced the worst day of the whole Uprising, maybe the worst day of all.

Antek came for us. Having lost its entire command in a house on Freta street. the remaining units of the AL were being evacuated through the sewers to Zoliborz. Antek came so that we could all go together, but we had to stay. We were alone with forty wounded whom we couldn't leave.

We parted, and in the hell of the dying Old Town it seemed that it would be a final parting.

On 29 September Wik Slawski took us to the manhole on Krasinski square. We were supposed to go through the sewers to the town centre and there to arrange places with the General Staff for the wounded from our hospital and then return to the Old Town for them. As we were supposed to come back, I left all of my precious things, including my photographs which I had taken with me from the ghetto. I had a small photograph of my mother in the pocket of my jumper and a five-dollar note sewn into the sleeve. And nothing else. I also left behind the money that remained from my work as a courier before the Uprising.

Then came the journey through the sewers. We were not the only ones. A string of people each clutching the person in front firmly by the arm or belt, so as not to get lost in the darkness, and deathly silence while passing under the manholes, crawling on all fours so as not to bump into hanging grenades. And the stench. Sewage pouring into your shoes. But we got through. We came out barefoot, and our dresses were not fit to wear. In the Command Post on Nowy Swiat we were issued some shoes, skirts and men's shirts. Apart from my jumper, that was all I had when the Uprising finished.

We didn't return to the Old Town. When, the next day, after having arranged places for our wounded, we went to the manhole, it turned out that the evacuation of the Old Town was already under way and that the passage in that direction was cut off. The next day our wounded came, but not all of them. Those who were wounded in the legs and who couldn't move stayed in the hospital on Miodowa street. When we went back there after the liberation, we found their charred bodies lying on beds in the basement.

Our billet in the town centre was the hospital on Mokotow-ska street at number 12, or 24, where we stayed until the end of the Uprising. The town centre differed from the Old Town in that it was a little easier to get water, but there was little food. We ate oats, which had been brought from a stable on Twarda street into which a tunnel had been dug. Many of the wounded starved to death.

It was a large hospital, both civilian and military. When the Uprising collapsed those who worked there were paid wages – twenty dollars a head – and given the choice of a prisoner of war camp together with the wounded soldiers, or a civilian camp in Pruszkow. Neither one nor the other suited us. We didn't want to give ourselves up to the Germans, and above all we wanted to look for our friends.

A fortunate combination of circumstances came to our aid. Looking for a way out, I went to the Red Cross. I saw a doctor being given a pass to get out of Warsaw with a group of wounded. It was a possible way out, but I had no documents apart from my identity card with a false surname. I don't really know what I expected when I went to the Medical Association on Koszykowa street. And there a near-miracle happened. At a desk in the office sat a secretary whom I had known well before the war. She had been a close acquaintance, almost a friend. She helped me. The director of the Association was still there. I obtained the papers of a member of the Association with my false surname, that is to say, I now had a doctor's identity card. (I still have it.) With these papers I went back to the Red Cross and obtained a pass for a nurse and twelve wounded, whom I was supposed to take to the Red Cross Hospital in Milanowek. The director of that hospital was Dr Skonieczny. We left Warsaw on 11 October 1944. Myself, Joanna, Wik Slawski, Wladek, with a group of partisans, and the wives of both of the doctors who had died in the Old Town. We arrived in Milanowek, where Dr Skonieczny put us up for the night.

The next day Joanna, Wladek and I separated from the rest of the group, who found shelter in the village of Falenty. We were thinking in terms of the future, that is, we believed in a miracle – finding the whole of our group which had gone to Zoliborz. After a few days of roughing it we managed to find a suitable flat in Grodzisko. Two rooms on the first floor, next to the loft, in which we arranged a shelter without any difficulty. There were Germans stationed on the ground floor. A unit of gendarmes, hunting for . . . resistance fighters.

It was Wladek's idea. It occurred to him that a friend of his from the University, a Ukrainian, lived in Grodzisko. He was a decent young man and a fairly good friend, who liked to drink. In return for a litre of vodka he gave us a document stating that both of us were Ukrainians, who had managed to escape after being arrested by . . . the resistance. We took this document to Czestochowa, where we had Ukrainian identity cards made for us in some Ukrainian Committee. We went to a Ukrainian priest and told him that we were married and obtained from him a Ukrainian wedding certificate. We now had a well-prepared "cover" for our flat, should we find our friends.

At this stage I should explain something which might seem unclear. At that time Wladek, with whom I had been through so much in the Uprising, was just a friend, who knew the secrets of my identity and work and who agreed to stay with

Starosta Grodzki
Warszawa-Północ

L.dz. 70/44

Warszawa, dnia 18.VIII.1944 r.

Tymczasowa legitymacja.

P, Dr. Meremińska Irena jest zatrudniona przy Starostwie Grodz-
kim Warszawa-Północ w charakterze lekarza pediatry i w związku z
tym upoważniona jest do poruszania się w terenie celem wykonywania
swej funkcji urzędowej.

Za Starostę Grodzkiego

/Dr.W.Skonieczny/
Lekarz Starostwa Grodzkiego

Document issued 18 August 1944 by the Local Council of North Warsaw

Temporary Identity

Dr Irena Mereminska is employed by the Local Council of North Warsaw in the capacity of paediatrician and is therefore authorized to travel in this region in the course of her duties.

Dr W. Skonieczny
Regional Medical Officer

The temporary pass issued by Dr W. Skonieczny in his capacity as Regional Medical Officer of North Warsaw, which allowed the author and thirteen companions to escape from the city after the collapse of the Warsaw Uprising. (*Adina Blady Szwajger*)

A.K.
D-wo Grupy „Północ"
Szef San.

Zaświadczenie

Niniejszym stwierdzam, iż Mereminińska Irena
pracowała w Szpitalu A.K.4 przy ul. Miodowej #24
od dnia 14. VIII 1944 r. do dnia 1 IX 1944 r.

A.K.
D-wo Grupy „Północ"
Szef San.

Wa 3 X 1944 r.

Certificate

I hereby state that Dr Irena Mereminska has worked in the hospital of the Home Army, 24 Miodowa street, from 12 July 1944 to 1 September 1944.

3.x.1944   *Chief Medical Officer of North Warsaw*

Certificate issued by the Home Army on 3 October 1944. (*Adina Blady Szwajger*) us and help us. I was not sure what would happen to us in the future. But I was free. I had said goodbye to Bernard just after the Uprising. He was taken over to the other side of the Vistula, to the liberated area, and after the war to the United States. We parted as close friends, but I didn't want to escape with him, although he had suggested it. And so I stayed with Wladek.

After this digression I return to the story of Grodzisko.

At the beginning of November 1944 two old ladies, friends of Tosia Goliborska, managed to find us. It turned out that after the fall of Zoliborz our friends had stayed in the cellar of a house on Promyka street in which Tosia had lived before the Uprising. This house was right next to the river Vistula. The Germans started to strengthen their defences on the Vistula. Our friends found themselves in danger of being discovered, and in any case had no food or water. The two old ladies had got out first to look for help. Now, we started to look for a way out. After a few days another two people managed to get out. I can't remember exactly who – Zosia? Marysia? Or someone else? It turned out that the situation was desperate. In the cellar they could already hear the sound of pickaxes and the voices of Germans.

We had to do something immediately! And we succeeded! The director of the hospital in Jelonki sent out a sanitary patrol. One of our girls went with them. I wasn't there, but I know that while walking across the minefield she took her shoes off, because it seemed to her that it would be safer in bare feet. The patrol managed to get to our friends and to lead them out. They put Marek on the stretcher, shouting to the Germans that he had *Fleckfieber* – typhus – which the Germans were very afraid of. Zygmunt, in a white coat, helped to carry the stretcher. The others went separately, carrying bundles, as though they had just been to loot the house. (There were already many such people around at that time.)

They came to our flat in Grodzisko, which now housed twelve people. Three of us were "legal", the rest were in hiding.

The three of us who had papers became so friendly with the gendarmes downstairs that they invited us for New Year's Eve.

They say that the darkest spot is under the lamp-post.

Apart from Marek and Antek, there were people from the Co-ordinating Committee of Jewish Organizations hiding in Milanowek, Pruszkow, Brwinow and in other places on the outskirts of Warsaw. Something had to be done. Our only activity at that time was keeping in touch with other centres, above all with Cracow, where life was relatively normal. I used to go to Cracow, sometimes on my own, sometimes accompanied by Wladek.

The war ended for us when on 18 January 1945 Polish and Soviet troops entered Grodzisko. What did we feel at that moment? I don't know. I know that we drank vodka that evening, probably because it seemed to be the appropriate thing to do. We had escaped with our lives – and that was all.

The next day we set out on foot for Warsaw. The journey took us four days. Eventually we arrived at the pile of rubble which had once been Warsaw.

The people from the hospital, that is, Marek, Zosia, Joanna and I, went straight away to Sienna street. The hospital was still standing. We hung a note on the entrance, "Hospital – Occupied", and then spent the night in an empty flat on Sienna street. What had we expected to achieve by hanging this naïve note? I don't know.

Next day we crossed the Vistula to Praga on the right bank. On 25 January 1945, I began to work for the Main Committee of Polish Jews as a paediatrician and the head of the child welfare unit.

My duties included finding children placed with Aryan families by our organization during the war, and digging them out of the shelters in which some of them had survived. I had to deal with children coming with their mothers as well. Some had survived in Warsaw and the others were brought by their mothers from other areas. None of these children was healthy and normal. On 15 May 1945, I

Wykaz dzieci znajdujących się u Aryjczyków

L.p.	Nazwisko i imię	Wiek	Nr rej.	Adres	Uwagi
1.	Passenstejn Daniel	l.6	15	11 Listopada 26/18	op. Salonek
2.	Altetwajn Gizella	l.4	48	Św. Wincentego 47	op. Pęgza.
3.	Margulis Mira	l.11	73	Grochowska 247/16	op. Ostucz.
4.	Feldman Rutti	l.9	74	Ossowska 52, 13	op. Chrzanowski
5.	Kraus Paweł	l.8	74	" " "	"
6.	Buchwald Halina	l.9	76	Saszczów 81/10	op. Stróżąca
7.	Szapiro Edita	l.8	151	Siennicka 15	Szpital
8.	Diment Artur	l.9	161	Śliwice-Wilkiewicza 33	op. Frankowska
9.	Rubin Henia	l.7	175	Pustelnik - Osiedle	op. H. Szczepański
10.	Langlewa Hasman Lazarz	l.8	252	Stalowa 35/10	op. Langiewicz
11.	Kornblum Boruch	l.12	289	Mińska 24	op. Dzgyński
12.	Kowalska Eugenia	l.4½	300	Grzyńszowa 6/42	op. Damska
13.	Goldman Stanisław	l.10	311	Grochów-Prochowa 22	op. Chmielczyk
14.	Kurc Krystyna	l.8	987	Grochowska 158/9	op. Wejcman
15.	Rubinsztajn Marysia	l.2	1076	Brzeska 10/26	op. Kałużyńska
16.	Lemberg Antoni	l.12	1148	Mackiewicza 1/4	op. Burno
17.	Kanarek Raja	l.13	1570	Wileńska 9	
18.	Rochman Józio	l.8	1586	Św. Augusta 1012	op. Dąbrowska
19.	Spiegel Bernard	l.5	1677	Bemiszewska 6	op. Piotrowska
20.	Gliklich Anna	l.7	1718	Targowa Dom dozorcy	op. Żurik
21.	Sztorchman Eurysja	l.12	1742	Gołowicki-graniczna 17	
22.	Kupersztch Marian	l.7	1824		
23.	Fajnsztajn Lili	l.9	1873	Wróbla 15, 135	op. Szymański
24.	Zaks Ewica	l.7	1855	Zielna Ujm...	op. ...

A record of Jewish children placed with Aryan families recovered from the rubble in the basement of a destroyed house, and used by the author to locate such children in the course of her duties for the Main Council of Polish Jews in the Spring of 1945. The headings read (from left to right): Name, Age, Registration number, address and name of Aryan family. (*Adina Blady Szwajger*) went to Lodz, where Dr Margolis with her family and Marek had gone already. I started to work in a sanatorium in Lagiewniki, near Lodz, under the supervision of Dr Margolis. Wladek, for the time being, stayed in Warsaw. I decided to specialize in tuberculosis in children. It seemed to me the closest thing to what I had done before. In the following few years I passed all my overdue exams and obtained a real medical diploma. I carried on working with children, specializing in chest disease.

Names I Remember

Antek (see Icchak Cukierman)

Blady Szwajger, Adina – Irena Mereminska – Junior Doctor – (survived)

Blum, Abrasza – one of the organizers of armed resistance in the ghetto, a member of the Co-ordinating Committee of Jewish Organizations

Blum-Bielicka, Luba – Head of the Nurses School; worked in the hospital on Gesia street

Braude-Heller, Dr Anna – Head Doctor at the Bersohn and Bauman Children's Hospital – (died in April 1943)

Cukierman, Icchak – Antek – member of the Co-ordinating Committee of Jewish Organizations; a member of the Command Staff of ZOB

Edelman, Marek – Hospital Runner for the Bersohn and Bauman Children's Hospital; on the Command Staff of ZOB – (survived)

Efros, Dr – Doctor – (died in Treblinka)

Fedentrumf, Dr – Head of the Infectious Diseases Ward – (died in Treblinka)

Feinmesser, Bronislawa (Bronka) – Marysia Warman – (living in the USA)

Ferszt, Fajga – Laboratory worker – (died in Majdanek)

Ferszt, Josef (Jozio) – Head Administrator – (died in Majdanek)

Fersztowna, Fecia – Laboratory worker; sister of Josef Ferszt

Folman, Dr Maria – Assistant Doctor on the Typhus Ward – (died in Treblinka)

Frakter, Dr Zosia – Doctor – (poisoned herself at the *Umschlag*)

Frydman, Renia – Zosia Skaszewska – (survived)

Goldman, Maria – Administrative secretary, Regina Goldman's sister – (died during the war)

Goldman, Regina – Office manager – (died after the war)

Goliborska-Golobowa, Teodozja (Tosia) – Head of the Laboratory – (survived; living in Australia)

Heller, Dr Anna (see Dr Anna Braude-Heller)

Heller, Arik – son of Dr Anna Braude-Heller and fellow student of Adina Blady Szwajger

Higber, Dr Luba – Doctor – (died in Treblinka)

Hirszfeld, Professor Hanna – Ward Head Doctor at Leszno street – (survived)

Hodes, Mrs – Head Cook – (survived; died in the USA)

Jaszunski, Dr Michal – Assistant Doctor on the Internal Diseases Ward at Leszno street – (died)

Jurek (see Arie Wilner)

Kachane-Kochanska, Dr – Assistant Doctor on the Infectious Diseases Ward – (died of natural causes after the war)

Keilson, Alexander – Leon Malecki – father of Hela and Dola Keilson

Keilson, Debora (Dola) – Matron – (shot in Otwock in 1943)

Keilson, Dr Helena (Hela) – Janina Malecka (later Pulawska) – Doctor on the Internal Diseases Ward – (survived the camps; living in Sweden)

Kelniec, Mirka – Nurse in the Operating Theatre – (died)

Klepfisz, Michal – engineer, organized the production of hand grenades and incendiary bottles in the ghetto – (died)

Kroszczor, Henryk – Administrative Director (died after the war)

Leneman, Dr – Assistant Doctor on the Surgical Ward – (died in Treblinka)

Lewin, Dr – Laryngologist – (survived)

Lichtenbaum, Dr – Head of the Internal Diseases Ward – (died in Treblinka)

Makower, Dr – Ward Doctor at Leszno street – (survived)

Malecka, Janina (see Hela Keilson)

Margolis, Dr Anna – Head of the Tuberculosis Ward (survived)

Natanblut-Heller, Marysia – childhood friend of Adina Blady Szwajger; married to Arik Heller

Natanblut-Heller, Halina – (caught in the round-up at the café on Miodowa street; shot in Pawiak prison)

Pulawska, Janina (see Hela Keilson)

Rajtazer, Symcha – Kazik – member of ZOB Command Staff

Rotbalsam, Dr Jerzy (Jurek) – Second Assistant Doctor on the Internal Diseases Ward (survived)

Rozowski, Stasia – wife of Welwl Rozowski

Rozowski, Welwl – Wlodek, – ZOB fighter

Rubni, Sara – Nurse on the Typhus Ward at Sliska street – (died)

Sachs, Mrs – Book keeper; doctor's widow – (died)

Skaszewska, Zosia (see Renia Frydman)

Skonieczny, Dr Waclaw (Wacek) – The Dean of the Hospital appointed by the Germans (survived; died after the war)

Slawski, Wik (see Wladyslaw Swidowski)

Swidowski, Wladyslaw – Wik Slawski – Resistance fighter with the Home Army – (Adina Blady-Szwajger's second husband)

Szpigielman, Stefan – the author's first husband

Szpigielman, Mieteck – Stefan Szpigielman's older brother

Tenenbaum, Mrs – House Nurse – (poisoned herself, leaving her "life ticket" to her daughter)

Trediakowski, Jerzy – Clerk from Lodz who supplied false documents to members of ZOB

Waclaw (see Henryk Wolinski)

Wagner-Lewin, Lilka – Nurse – (survived)

Warman, Marysia (see Bronislawa [Bronka] Feinmesser)

Wilk, Dr – Head Surgeon – (survived; emigrated to Sweden)

Wilk, Dr – Doctor; ophthalmological consultant – (wife of the above; survived; emigrated to Sweden)

Wilner, Arie – Jurek – Courier for Zegota on the "Aryan side"

Wladek (see Welwl Rozowski)

Wolinski, Henryk – Waclaw – in charge of Jewish Affairs for the Home Army's Chief Command

Zerebianka, Maria (Maniysia) – friend of Adina Blady Szwajger's mother

Documents of the Warsaw Ghetto

HISTORY

Dawidowicz, Lucy S.: *The War Against the Jews 1933–45*, Harmondsworth, 1975.

Dawidowicz, Lucy S., Ed.: *A Holocaust Reader*, New York, 1976.

Gilbert, Martin: *The Holocaust: The Jewish Tragedy*, London, 1986.

Gutman, Yisrael: *The Jews of Warsaw 1939–43. Ghetto, Underground, Revolt*, Brighton, 1982.

Goldstein, Bernard: *The Stars Bear Witness*, New York, 1949.

Grossman, Mendel: *With a Camera in the Ghetto*, Ghetto Fighters' House, Israel, 1970.

Edelman, Marek: *The Ghetto Fights*, New York, 1946.

Lewin, Nora: *The Holocaust: The Destruction of the European Jewry, 1933–45*, New York, 1968.

Friedman, Philip: *Martyrs and Fighters. The Epic of the Warsaw Ghetto*, New York, 1954.

Bartoszewski, Wladyslaw and Lewin, Zofia: *Righteous Among Nations: How Poles Helped the Jews, 1939–45*, London, 1969.

Ainsztein, R.: *The Warsaw Ghetto, Revolt*, New York, 1979.

Robinson, J., Ed., *The Holocaust and After: Sources and Literature in English*, Jerusalem, 1973.

DIARIES AND MEMOIRS

Adler, Stanislaw: *In the Warsaw Ghetto 1940–43, An Account of a Witness*, Jerusalem, 1982.

Bauman, Janina: *Winter in the Morning*, London, 1986.

Berg, Mary: *Warsaw Ghetto; A Diary by Mary Berg*, Ed. S. L. Schneiderman, New York, 1945.

The Warsaw Diary of Adam Czerniakow: Prelude to Doom, Ed. Raul

Hilberg, Stanislaw Staron and Josef Kermish, New York, 1979.

The Warsaw Diary of Chaim A. Kaplan, Trans. and ed. Abraham Katsch, New York, 1973.

Krall, Hanna: *Shielding the Flame: an Intimate Conversation with Marek Edelman*, New York, 1986.

Lewin, Abraham: *A Cup of Tears: A Diary of the Warsaw Ghetto*, Oxford, 1988.

Litai, Chaim Lazar: *Muranowska 7: The Warsaw Ghetto Rising*, Tel Aviv, 1968.

Meed, Wladka (Miedzyrzecki): *On Both Sides of the Wall: Memoirs from the Warsaw Ghetto*, Beit Lohamei Hagettaot, 1972.

Ringelblum, Emanuel: *Notes from the Warsaw Ghetto*, New York, 1958.

Wdowinski, David: *And We Are Not Saved*, London, 1964.

Zydelberg, Michael: *A Warsaw Diary 1939–45*, London, 1969.

Donat, A.: *The Holocaust Kingdom. A Memoir*, New York, 1965.

Zucker-Bojanowska, L.: *Liliana's Journal: Warsaw 1939–45*, New York, 1980.

PHOTOGRAPHS

Heydecker, Joe J.; *The Warsaw Ghetto: a Photographic Record 1941 –44*, Foreword by Heinrich Böll, London, 1990.

Keller, Ulrich, Ed.: *The Warsaw Ghetto in Photographs. 206 views*, Toronto, 1984.

Szajkowski, Z.: *An Illustrated Sourcebook of the Holocaust*, 3 vols., New York, 1977.

The Warsaw Ghetto in Pictures, Illustrated Catalogue, YIVO, New York, 1970.

Warszawskie Getto, 1943–1988, W45 Rocznice Powstania, Wyawnictwo Interpress, Warsaw, 1988.